D1450520

Modern Critical Views

Modern Critical Views

Katherine Mansfield
Christopher Marlowe
Andrew Marvell
Herman Melville
George Meredith
James Merrill
John Stuart Mill
Arthur Miller
Henry Miller
John Milton
Yukio Mishima
Molière
Michel de Montaigne
Eugenio Montale
Marianne Moore
Alberto Moravia
Toni Morrison
Alice Munro
Iris Murdoch
Robert Musil
Vladimir Nabokov
V. S. Naipaul
R. K. Narayan
Pablo Neruda
John Henry Newman
Friedrich Nietzsche
Frank Norris
Joyce Carol Oates
Sean O'Casey
Flannery O'Connor
Christopher Okigbo
Charles Olson
Eugene O'Neill
José Ortega y Gasset
Joe Orton
George Orwell
Ovid
Wilfred Owen
Amos Oz
Cynthia Ozick
Grace Paley
Blaise Pascal
Walter Pater
Octavio Paz
Walker Percy
Petrarch
Pindar
Harold Pinter
Luigi Pirandello
Sylvia Plath
Plato

Plautus
Edgar Allan Poe
Poets of Sensibility & the
  Sublime
Poets of the Nineties
Alexander Pope
Katherine Anne Porter
Ezra Pound
Anthony Powell
Pre-Raphaelite Poets
Marcel Proust
Manuel Puig
Alexander Pushkin
Thomas Pynchon
Francisco de Quevedo
François Rabelais
Jean Racine
Ishmael Reed
Adrienne Rich
Samuel Richardson
Mordecai Richler
Rainer Maria Rilke
Arthur Rimbaud
Edwin Arlington Robinson
Theodore Roethke
Philip Roth
Jean-Jacques Rousseau
John Ruskin
J. D. Salinger
Jean-Paul Sartre
Gershom Scholem
Sir Walter Scott
William Shakespeare
  Histories & Poems
  Comedies & Romances
  Tragedies
George Bernard Shaw
Mary Wollstonecraft
  Shelley
Percy Bysshe Shelley
Sam Shepard
Richard Brinsley Sheridan
Sir Philip Sidney
Isaac Bashevis Singer
Tobias Smollett
Alexander Solzhenitsyn
Sophocles
Wole Soyinka
Edmund Spenser
Gertrude Stein
John Steinbeck

Stendhal
Laurence Sterne
Wallace Stevens
Robert Louis Stevenson
Tom Stoppard
August Strindberg
Jonathan Swift
John Millington Synge
Alfred, Lord Tennyson
William Makepeace Thackeray
Dylan Thomas
Henry David Thoreau
James Thurber and S. J.
  Perelman
J. R. R. Tolkien
Leo Tolstoy
Jean Toomer
Lionel Trilling
Anthony Trollope
Ivan Turgenev
Mark Twain
Miguel de Unamuno
John Updike
Paul Valéry
Cesar Vallejo
Lope de Vega
Gore Vidal
Virgil
Voltaire
Kurt Vonnegut
Derek Walcott
Alice Walker
Robert Penn Warren
Evelyn Waugh
H. G. Wells
Eudora Welty
Nathanael West
Edith Wharton
Patrick White
Walt Whitman
Oscar Wilde
Tennessee Williams
William Carlos Williams
Thomas Wolfe
Virginia Woolf
William Wordsworth
Jay Wright
Richard Wright
William Butler Yeats
A. B. Yehoshua
Emile Zola

Modern Critical Views

ROBERT LOWELL

Edited and with an introduction by

Harold Bloom
Sterling Professor of the Humanities
Yale University

CHELSEA HOUSE PUBLISHERS
New York ◇ Philadelphia

Library of Congress Cataloging-in-Publication Data
Robert Lowell.
    (Modern critical views)
    Bibliography: p.
    Includes index.
    Summary: A collection of critical essays on Lowell
and his works arranged in chronological order of
publication.
    1. Lowell, Robert, 1917–1977—Criticism and
interpretation. [1. Lowell, Robert, 1917–1977—
Criticism and interpretation.   2. American poetry—
History and criticism]   I. Bloom, Harold.   II. Series.
PS3523.089Z853   1986   811'.52   86-20737
ISBN 0-87754-629-0

Contents

Editor's Note

This book gathers what is, in my judgment, a representative selection of the most useful criticism devoted to the poetry of Robert Lowell, arranged in the chronological order in which the reviews and critical essays first appeared. I am grateful to Jennifer Wagner for her erudition and insight in helping to edit this volume.

My introduction, indubitably the most disenchanted critical response in this collection, begins with an overview of Lowell's final book, and then attempts a canonical judgment as to Lowell's earlier work in *Lord Weary's Castle*. The chronological sequence begins with a retrospective view of *Land of Unlikeness*, Lowell's first book, by Hugh B. Staples, who finds the Manichean rhetoric of religious violence prophetic of better poems to come.

The acidulous John Simon, reviewing the three one-act plays that constitute *The Old Glory*, concludes that Lowell's poetry was better kept off stage. Gabriel Pearson, surveying Lowell's middle phase in *Life Studies* and *For the Union Dead*, defends their apparent informality as an aspect of an overt design. Rather differently, David Bromwich questions whether *Notebook* is anything but bad verse, and implies that the book is transitional work at best.

Lowell's poetic politics are analyzed by Dwight Eddins, for whom *Near the Ocean*, with its sense of political realities and human weakness, is more credible than the idealizing dreams of Lowell's earlier work. Frances Ferguson, charting Lowell's verse through the *Notebooks*, shrewdly questions whether the poet ever gets beyond trivializing historical time.

Imitations is lucidly investigated by Stephen Yenser, who wonders whether Lowell has kept the structure of the book from fading into the texture of allusions. More positively, David Kalstone defends Lowell's work through *For the Union Dead* by insisting "that autobiography for Lowell is a problematic form" and indeed is written by him from an elegist's point of view.

A more vehement defense of *Day by Day* is formidably made by Helen

Vendler, who goes so far as to compare Lowell's poetry of old age to Whitman's and to Stevens's, a judgment that is very generous indeed. More descriptively, Steven Gould Axelrod chronicles the influence of William Carlos Williams on *Life Studies*, while Neil Corcoran finds the "grandeur of imperfection" in *The Dolphin*.

In this book's final essay, Bruce Michelson returns to *Lord Weary's Castle* in order to trace the effect of Randall Jarrell's critical advice upon the making of that book. The differences, in approach and in judgment, between Michelson's comments upon "The Quaker Graveyard in Nantucket" and the Johnsonian observations I have permitted myself in my introduction, should stimulate the reader to arrive at her or his own estimate of that poem, and of Lowell's problematic achievement in general.

Introduction

I

Robert Lowell's final volume, *Day by Day* (1977), has about it the particular poignance that attends a last performance, a display of things in their farewell. The book's most ambitious poem, "Ulysses and Circe," seeks to elevate heroic wryness into a kind of sublimity, as when Ulysses-Lowell observes of himself: "He dislikes everything / in his impoverished life of myth." But the poetic impoverishment becomes more the burden, throughout the volume, than does the overt sorrow of personal mythology. A curious flatness or deadness of tone, indubitably achieved by considerable artistry, works against the expressive strength of the poet's struggle with tradition. The best poems in the book, upon rereading, seem to me the last four, where the pathos dares to become overwhelming, turning as it does upon the poet's reading of his life's losses as being the consequences of his mother's rejection. Yet I am left uncertain as to whether I am not being moved by a record of human suffering, rather than by a making of any kind. Lowell prays for "the grace of accuracy" and comes to rest upon the poetically self-defeating question: "Yet why not say what happened?"

From *Life Studies* (1959) on, Lowell took up his own revisionary version of William Carlos Williams's rhetorical stance as a defense against his own precursors, T. S. Eliot and Allen Tate. This stance, which is in Williams a fiction of nakedness, becomes in Lowell the trope of vulnerability. The trope, once influential and fashionable, has become the mark of a school of poets who now seem writers of period pieces: the "Confessional" school of Anne Sexton, Sylvia Plath, the earlier W. D. Snodgrass, the later work of John Berryman. "Confessional" verse, intended to be revelatory, soon seemed opaque. One read a poem even by Lowell or Berryman and concluded that both poet and reader knew less about poet and reader than they did before the poem was written and read. By a profound paradox, it became clear that a guarded, reticent meditation like Stevens's "The Poems of Our Climate" could yield endless knowledge of both the poet and oneself, whereas Lowell's overtly candid "Waking in the Blue" or "Man and Wife" simply impoverished all knowing whatsoever.

Time therefore seems to have darkened Lowell's aura in the decade since his death. Elizabeth Bishop is now firmly established as the enduring artist of Lowell's generation, since the canonical sequence of our poetry seems to many among us, myself included, to move from Stevens through Bishop on to James Merrill and John Ashbery, whose extraordinary works of the last decade are a range beyond anything in Lowell or Berryman. Lowell's legacy continues in the verse of poets as diverse as Adrienne Rich and Allen Grossman, but counts perhaps for rather less than seemed likely a decade ago.

II

Lowell's early poems, in *Land of Unlikeness* (1944) and *Lord Weary's Castle* (1946), would appear to be the most authentic expressions of his characteristic sensibility. The "fierce Latinity" of Allen Tate reverberates in these Eliotic poems, written and published in the heyday of the New Criticism, the Eliot-inspired, neo-Christian, ironic formalism of Tate, Cleanth Brooks, Robert Penn Warren, R. P. Blackmur, and the other mandarins of an anti-Romantic polemical sect. The early Lowell is the most considerable of the poets schooled by the New Critics into a verse tense with impasse, deploring the present and celebrating an imaginative past that excluded Wordsworth and Whitman, the actual founders of modern Anglo-American poetry. Setting the remote figure of John Donne over the perpetual immediacy of William Wordsworth, echoing the diction and cadences of the self-baffled Gerard Manley Hopkins rather than the prophetic rhetoric of Walt Whitman, Lowell arrived at a mode queerly similar, as David Bromwich has observed, to the American metaphysical verse of the Puritan Edward Taylor, whose courageous attempt to accommodate a baroque sensibility to the American wilderness finds a late, plangent echo in the Boston apocalypses of *Lord Weary's Castle*.

I remember once remarking to Lowell that my favorite among his earlier poems was "The Drunken Fisherman," an observation that did not please him, but forty years after first reading it, a return to the piece still finds it an eloquent and adequate reflection of the Jacobean temper of Webster and Tourneur as mediated by the revisionary ironies of Eliot and Tate:

> A calendar to tell the day;
> A handkerchief to wave away

> The gnats; a couch unstuffed with storm
> Pouching a bottle in one arm;
> A whiskey bottle full of worms;
> And bedroom slacks: are these fit terms
> To mete the worm whose molten rage
> Boils in the belly of old age?

All the benign charms of Eliot's visions of Sweeney or of Tate's "Æneas at Washington" are condensed into this New Critical performance piece. We have a portrait of St. Peter as Webster's Bosola and Flamineo or Tourneur's Vindice might have seen him:

> Is there no way to cast my hook
> Out of this dynamited brook?
> The Fisher's sons must cast about
> When shallow waters peter out.
> I will catch Christ with a greased worm,
> And when the Prince of Darkness stalks
> My bloodstream to its Stygian term . . .
> On water the Man-Fisher walks.

I think sometimes that my favorite couplet of and about the Eliotic school and its dilemmas must be this, from that pungent stanza:

> The Fisher's sons must cast about
> When shallow waters peter out.

The pun in "peter out" may stand as a representative instance of this school of wit.

The most ambitious poems in *Lord Weary's Castle* are the seven part elegy, "The Quaker Graveyard in Nantucket," and "Where the Rainbow Ends," a vision of the Last Things. Rereading "The Quaker Graveyard" just now, on Martha's Vineyard, two hours by ferry from Nantucket, on a stormy day, I have conceived an esteem for the poem in excess of my previous judgment. Perhaps Lowell attempted too much in writing his own "Lycidas," so to speak, a little too early, and the excessive number of overt references to *Moby-Dick* insistently invite comparisons that do not make Melville shrink. But Lowell at least found fit matter for his baroque rhetoric:

> When the whale's viscera go and the roll
> Of its corruption overruns this world
> Beyond tree-swept Nantucket and Wood's Hole
> And Martha's Vineyard, Sailor, will your sword

Whistle and fall and sink into the fat?
In the great ash-pit of Jehoshaphat
The bones cry for the blood of the white whale,
The fat flukes arch and whack about its ears,
The death-lance churns into the sanctuary, tears
The gun-blue swingle, heaving like a flail,
And hacks the coiling life out: it works and drags
And rips the sperm-whale's midriff into rags,
Gobbets of blubber spill to wind and weather,
Sailor, and gulls go round the stoven timbers
Where the morning stars sing out together
And thunder shakes the white surf and dismembers
The red flag hammered in the mast-head. Hide,
Our steel, Jonas Messias, in Thy side.

The last line, with its suggestion that the Eliotic school favored Jonah, more even as Messiah than as fleeing prophet, is not inaccurate, though the appropriation of Job's great trope of the morning stars singing out together is rather too bold. Lowell's early diction, rarely subdued, may be said to have attained its apotheosis in "Where the Rainbow Ends," not so much perhaps one of the poems of our climate as it is redolent of Eliot's ideological waste land:

I saw the sky descending, black and white,
Not blue, on Boston where the winters wore
The skulls to jack-o'-lanterns on the slates,
And Hunger's skin-and-bone retrievers tore
The chickadee and shrike. The thorn tree waits
Its victim and tonight
The worms will eat the deadwood to the foot
Of Ararat: the scythers, Time and Death,
Helmed locusts, move upon the tree of breath;
The wild ingrafted olive and the root.

As an instance of what must, I suppose, be called the poetry of belief, this is by no means wasted, since it does mark one of the limits of Modernist rhetoric in our time. If Eliot is, as I would suspect, the Abraham Cowley of our age, and Ezra Pound its John Cleveland or Edmund Waller, then the early Lowell may justly dispute with Allen Tate the position of our William Mason, once renowned for the vigor and flamboyance of his Pindaricks.

HUGH B. STAPLES

Land of Unlikeness

Such is the condition of those who live in the Land of Unlikeness. They are not happy there. Wandering, hopelessly revolving, in the "circuit of the impious" those who tread this weary round suffer not only the loss of God but also the loss of themselves. They dare no longer look their own souls in the face; could they do it they would no longer recognize themselves. For when the soul has lost its likeness to God it is no longer like itself: inde anima dissimilis Deo, inde dissimilis est et sibi; *a likeness which is no longer like its original is like itself no more.*
—ETIENNE GILSON, *The Mystical Theology of Saint Bernard*

Land of Unlikeness reflects a mind deeply preoccupied with the alienation of the human soul from the Mind of God. The title is taken from St. Bernard, but ultimately derives from St. Augustine's metaphor *regio dissimilitudinis* for the agony of a soul still held captive by the world of the senses yet sufficiently aware of God to perceive the dark strangeness of the material world and the falsity of mortal existence pursued for its own sake. The spiritual consequences of such inchoate awareness are emphasized by the book's epigraph, *Inde anima dissimilis Deo inde dissimilis est et sibi*, from St. Bernard's sermons of the Song of Songs; the phrase has for modern readers the suggestion of psychological schism as well. The Lowell of *Land of Unlikeness*, like the Eliot of *The Waste Land* before him, portrays the nightmare of contemporary culture, made specially vivid by the holocaust of World War II. It records the quest of a Christian for religious security against a background of chaos, disorder and destruction.

In the twenty-one poems of Lowell's first volume, revelation and hal-

From *Robert Lowell: The First Twenty Years.* © 1962 by Hugh B. Staples. Farrar, Straus & Cudahy, 1962.

lucination merge. He consistently evokes the grotesque, as in "The Crucifix," where he overcomes a mood of religious despair by rejecting Adam and his legacy of Original Sin in these terms:

> Get out from under my feet, old man. Let me pass;
> On Ninth Street through the Hallowe'en's soaped glass
> I picked at an old Bone on two crossed sticks
> And found, to *Via et Vita et Veritas*
> A stray dog's signpost is a crucifix.

The pervasive tone of these spiritual exercises is sombre and violent; the emphasis is on the Dark Night of the Soul rather than the Light of Salvation, on an awareness of Evil rather than a celebration of the power of Good. And although the ritual quality of some of the poems, reflected in such titles as "On the Eve of the Feast of the Immaculate Conception, 1942," evidences the piety and gravity with which they are conceived, there remains a substratum of doubt, an apprehension that God's patience may at last be exhausted and the promise of Salvation withdrawn. Throughout, there is a fascination, almost Manichean in its intensity, with the power of Evil. Perhaps the keynote to *Land of Unlikeness* is supplied by the frontispiece, which pictures not a conventional crucifix, but a gargoyle hanging from the Cross. The symbolism of this device, like that of many of the poems, seems deliberately ambiguous as if to suggest on the one hand the triumph of Christianity over Satan, and on the other the modern displacement of spiritual values, wherein not Christ but the power of Evil is elevated as an object of worship.

In a review of *Four Quartets*, Lowell wrote: "My own feeling is that union with God is somewhere in sight in all poetry, though it is usually rudimentary and misunderstood." While it is true that all of the *Land of Unlikeness* poems, even the inventions on historical themes such as "Napoleon Crosses the Berezina" and "Dea Roma" have a religious context, the intensity and direction of religious force vary a good deal from poem to poem. As R. P. Blackmur puts it: "in dealing with men his faith compels him to be fractiously vindictive, and in dealing with faith, his experience of men compels him to be nearly blasphemous." The greater number of these poems are impersonal and apocalyptic; they are set in a contemporary, sometimes topical framework in which the spectacle of mass destruction stands in dramatic contrast to the teachings of the Church. Some, however, dwell on earlier evidence of man's inhumanity to man drawn from the history of New England. Thus in such poems as "Children of Light" and "The Park Street Cemetery" (later expanded and more trenchantly entitled "At the Indian Killer's Grave") Lowell deals not with the predicament of a world that has ceased trying to attain union with God, but with a culture even more hopelessly damned—a society that committed atrocities in the name of a false creed—the Calvinism of the Puritan theocracy. In two poems, Lowell strikes a personal rather than a professional pose: "A Suicidal Nightmare" and "The Drunken Fisherman," but in both cases the opportunity for purely lyrical expression is somewhat obscured by a heavy coating of melodrama; indeed, it is only in his latest poems in *Life Studies* that personal experience is recorded with clarity and frankness. All three of these subjects—the gloomy lamentations over the world conflict, the satiric probing of the spiritual malignancies in the history of New England, and the exploitation of personal anguish, are integrated in only one poem, "In Memory of Arthur Winslow." This elegy to his grandfather is the finest of all Lowell's early poems and merits a full discussion later in this [essay].

For Lowell, the war seems to have been Armageddon; to his poetic vision, as to Blake's, the appurtenances of an industrial civilization are accommodated directly into a general allegory: bombers become destroying angels, warships are Leviathans. Cain and Abel, Adam, Mars, Bellona, Satan and even the Virgin appear as contenders in the cosmic field while the issue hangs in doubt. In his personal career, Lowell's attitude towards the war ranged from vain attempts to enlist to an obdurate defiance of authority that ended in his imprisonment. Something of this ambivalence is felt in the dozen religious interpretations of the hostilities: their difficulty owes as much to a lack of consistent viewpoint as to the unexpected application of allusion and the curious air of colloquial intimacy with which the mythological and divine antagonists are addressed. Thus it is sometimes impossible to separate Lowell's anger and despair from his irony and satire.

In the opening stanza, for example, of "On the Eve of the Feast of the Immaculate Conception, 1942," the attempt to yoke the Virgin with Mars and Bellona seems to be a satiric indictment of Christian militancy, and the odd, shocking epithet "burly" reinforces the apparent mood of bitter jest:

> Mother of God, whose burly love
> Turns swords to plowshares, come, improve
>   On the big wars
> And make this holiday with Mars
> Your Feast Day, while Bellona's bluff
> Courage or call it what you please
>   Plays blindman's buff
>   Through virtue's knees.

Yet the poem goes on to deplore the Virgin's failure to intercede in the hostilities. Citing the medieval tradition of her victory over Satan, the poet invokes her aid in these pungent terms:

Oh, if soldiers mind you well
They shall find you are their belle
    And belly too;
Christ's bread and beauty came by you,
Celestial Hoyden, when our Lord
Gave up the weary Ghost and died,
    You shook a sword
    From his torn side.

Over the seas and far away
They feast the fair and bloody day
    When mankind's Mother,
Jesus' Mother, like another
Nimrod danced on Satan's head.
The old Snake lopes to his shelled hole;
    Man eats the Dead
    From pole to pole.

The language here reflects in part a young poet's conscious striving for
novelty; it is barely rescued from bathos by the dignity and strength of the
religious emotion that produced it. In these poems, the quasi-facetious man-
ner is usually balanced by the sincerity of the poet's faith. This kind of
contradiction is likewise demonstrated in "The Boston Nativity," in which
Lowell attacks the empty, decadent "unchristian carollings" sung by Beacon
Hill revellers on Christmas Eve:

"Peace and goodwill on earth"
Liberty Bell rings out with its cracked clang.
If Baby asks for gifts at birth,
    Santa will hang
Bones of democracy
Upon the Christmas Tree.

Yet surprisingly the poem ends on a note of faith that counteracts the earlier
tone of cynicism:

Jesus, the Maker of this holiday,
Ungirds his loins' eternal clay.

A similar contrast is developed in "The Bomber." After picturing the Bomber
as a symbol of *hybris*, the poet prophesies mankind's impotence in the Day
of Judgment, an event always imminent in the *Land of Unlikeness*:

> O Bomber your wings are furled
> And your choked engines coast.
> The Master has had enough
> Of your trial flights and your cops
> And robbers and blindman's buff
> And Heaven's purring stops
> *When Christ gives up the ghost.*

In the remainder of the war poems, "Scenes from the Historic Comedy," "The Crucifix," "The Wood of Life," "Christmas Eve in Time of War," "Cistercians in Germany," and "Leviathan," Lowell's partisan enthusiasms are modified by his insistence on seeing the human conflict as of minor importance. The events taking place around him are merely reflections of the greater cosmic conflict; international warfare is viewed as a footnote to the story of Cain and Abel; military disasters are rehearsals for the impending Day of Judgment. In a sense, Lowell implies, human history does not matter any more—perhaps God has his mind on larger matters.

Under the surface decoration of these poems, behind the ritual and the conventional symbolism, lies the agony of doubt. The petitions to the Virgin, the religious meditations, the assertions of faith are shot through with an obsessive blood-guilt. And on a formal level, the intricate patterns contrast with the tone of violence and the disruptive force of blunt, clanging imagery; indeed, this central conflict between order and destruction lends these poems their chief distinction. For example, in "Dea Roma," Lowell begins in an easy, Audenesque conversational manner which heightens the violence of his theme:

> Augustus mended you. He hung the tongue
> Of Tullius upon your rostrum, lashed
> The money-lenders from your Senate House;
> Then Brutus bled his forty-six percent
> For *Pax Romana*. Quiet as a mouse
> Blood licks your Greek cosmetics with its tongue.

The device, though effective, is a perilous one; occasionally the force of Lowell's indignation bursts through even the most severe metrical restraints; the effect is no longer colloquial, but desperate and breathless, as of a man shouting at the top of his lungs. Thus, in "Christ for Sale," no amount of carefully premeditated rhyming can rescue his indictment of religious exploitation from prosaic vulgarity:

> In Greenwich Village, Christ the Drunkard brews
> Gall, or spiked bone-vat, siphons His bilged blood
> Into weak brain-pans and unseasons wood:
> His auctioneers are four hog-fatted Jews.
> In furs and bundlings of vitality,
> Cur ladies, ho, swill down the ichor in this Dye.

Altogether, Lowell is trying too hard here; his disgust for the "loitering carrion," as he calls them in his final stanza, is deeply felt, no question about that, but the total effect remains emetic rather than aesthetic. The last line in particular is a bold experiment in cacophony, but it betrays a youthful partiality for rhetorical exaggeration where restraint is needed, and a disturbing insensitivity to rhythm that is by no means completely absent in even the later work. Few poets are as uneven in this respect: often in a single poem Lowell is capable of such imaginatively rendered images as this from "A Suicidal Nightmare":

> A wooly lava of abstractions, flowed
> Over my memory's inflated bag.

only to sink to the flat prose of the concluding lines:

> "Brother, I fattened a caged beast on blood
> And knowledge had let the cat out of the bag."

Similar infelicities mar "The Boston Nativity," "Scenes from the Historic Comedy," and "The Wood of Life," where the comic effect of the double-rhyme of

> Here are scales whose Reckoning-weight
> Outweighs the apple's fell dejection;
> Our cornerstone, the Jews' Rejection

can hardly have been intended in this solemn celebration of Good Friday. Again, in "Satan's Confession," Lowell's conception of our original parent as a kind of gross *rentier* has a certain shock value but his language is bathetic:

> Adam, you idle-rich
> Image of the Divine:
>   Tell me, what holds your hand?
>   Fat of the land.
> My wife's a bitch;
> My Garden is Love's Shrine

To be sure, we may overlook the offence to decorum, but when the grotesque becomes merely farcical, the force of the poem as a whole is irretrievably diminished.

Like Eliot and Pound, Lowell is preoccupied with a sense of loss that results from contrasting the promise of the past to the futility of the present. The alienation of man from God, which I take to be the central theme of all the poems in *Land of Unlikeness*, finds its most dramatic expression for Lowell in the failure and death of the Puritan tradition. Perhaps in "Children of Light" he has in mind his own ancestors, one of whom, Josiah Winslow, was commander-in-chief of the colonial forces in King Philip's War:

> Our Fathers wrung their bread from stocks and stones
> And fenced their gardens with the Redman's bones;
> Embarking from the Nether Land of Holland,
> Pilgrims unhoused by Geneva's night,
> You planted here the Serpent's seeds of light;
> And here the pivoting searchlights probe to shock
> The riotous glass houses built on rock,
> And candles gutter in a hall of mirrors,
> And light is where the ancient blood of Cain
> Is burning, burning the unburied grain.

Lowell's use of paradox here reminds one of John Donne. By a reversal of the normal connotations of "light" and "dark" he provides an ironic comment on the parable of the unjust steward in Luke 16 ("And the Lord commended the unjust steward because he had done wisely; for the children of this world are wiser in their generation than the children of light"). Something too of Donne's fondness for word-play can be seen in the deliberate pun "the Nether Land of Holland." Again, as in many of Donne's poems, "Children of Light" is constructed upon a central paradox. The first five lines sum up the past; they represent the pious but misguided Puritan fathers whose material hardships in the Bay Colony are paralleled by the more important failure of false doctrine to provide spiritual nourishment: they are the "Pilgrims unhoused by Geneva's night." The second five lines juxtapose the present, in which the crime of Cain committed by the Puritans against the Indians has become enormously magnified into the holocaust of World War II. Ironically, the force of the Founding Fathers' religious zeal has been reduced to vain and illusory ritual. The single-minded pursuit of Mammon has vitiated piety; abundance has become excess and the surplus wheat cannot be consumed.

In "The Park Street Cemetery," Lowell contrasts the bright dreams of the Pilgrim ("The stocks and Paradises of the Puritan Dracos / New World eschatologies / That fascinated like a Walpurgis Nacht") to the shabby Boston of the present, "Where the Irish hold the Golden Dome." Similarly, the sonnets to Concord and Salem, symbols of New England's past intellectual and mercantile glory, are heavily imbued with images of paralysis and death: Concord, with its "ruined Bridge and Walden's fished-out perch," and Salem, where "Sea-sick spindrift drifts or skips / To the canvas flapping on the seaward panes" and "sewage sickens the rebellious seas." These early poems prefigure the apocalyptic destruction of Boston, the New Babylon, envisioned in "As a Plane Tree by the Water" and "Where the Rainbow Ends" of *Lord Weary's Castle*.

Lowell's indictment of the Protestant ethic and his portrayal of the consequences of its deterioration into mere materialism derive, then, from his general preoccupation with the spiritual vacuity of the present. His disapprobation of the things of this world and of the pagan energy of those who mistakenly pursue them finds its richest expression in the fine elegy to his grandfather, "In Memory of Arthur Winslow." Here Lowell displays, in a sustained effort, his astonishing ability to move with ease from the moral geography of Boston, capital of the *Land of Unlikeness*, to the cosmic scene, in which symbolism drawn from both Christian and pagan traditions are harmoniously fused.

As in many of Lowell's poems, we begin with a specific locale—Phillips House (the private, expensive division of the Massachusetts General Hospital), the Union Boat Club; in the second section, the Stark cemetery in Dunbarton, New Hampshire; Columbus, Ohio, in the third; and Copley Square in the fourth. From these still points in the turning world, there is a movement in the direction of the transcendental: from Charles River to the Acheron; from Copley Square to Heaven and Hell. But the Public Gardens, reserved in Lowell's boyhood for the *élite* are now desecrated by the "mid-Sunday Irish"; and in "Dunbarton" even the stones, the rocks of ages are cleft, and like the tradition they commemorate, subject to dissolution.

We find in part 3 that Grandfather Winslow has sought for permanence in the backward look at the family's historical achievement, but his compulsion to revive the past and make it meaningful in terms of the present has only led him to pursue an *ignis fatuus*: the power of gold. In his passionate attachment to the phenomenal world, Arthur Winslow has dissipated his spiritual capacities to the point where:

> the coxes' squeakings dwarf
> The *resurrexit Dominus* of all the bells.

The language of the Vulgate remains for him literally an unknown tongue; this is the reason why the poet, in his role as mediator, puts the words from the *Miserere* (slightly altered from *me* to an inclusive *nos*) into Latin:

Lavabis nos et super nivem dealbabor

in his effort to effect a kind of posthumous conversion. For Grandfather Winslow, the beautiful stained glass windows in the Protestant Trinity Church represent the limits of his spiritual imagination, just as they do for Villon's mother in the famous prayer he wrote for her—a ballade on which this section is based. The painted paradise symbolizes ceremony without faith, doomed to sink like Atlantis into the Devil's jaw.

Throughout the poem runs a dialectic of past and present, in which the past, or history is favourably compared to the present. Ultimately, however, the sordidness of the present vitiates even the nobility of the past. Thus in the second section, Lowell's own ancestors are rejected and subdued by "the minister, Kingsolving." Their day is gone; the envisioned greatness of the Puritan theocracy has not fulfilled its promise. The memory of their deeds, and their artefacts, remain as a kind of monument to misguided zeal, but their example is of no help to the living. Going further than this, in the final section Lowell, projecting his own spiritual development, tries to explain that it is precisely the operation of history, in terms of the family mercantile tradition (the "clippers and the slavers") that has prevented his grandfather from attaining grace. The narrow limits of Calvinism, with its vision of Paradise as harps and lutes, with its doctrine of election ("Kingsolving's church" becomes "the costly church" in the *Lord Weary's Castle* revision) has precluded the necessary apprehension of the transcendent power of God's mercy. All that is left for the poet is to pray for absolution through the Blood of the Lamb.

The final impression one retains from a reading of *Land of Unlikeness* is one of gravity. There are blemishes in these poems, nearly all of them stemming from a lack of sense of proportion. Yet Lowell's concern is cosmic; it is as though he were engaged in adapting the book of *Revelation* to a contemporary framework, and it is no wonder that the book as a whole is marked by a complete absence of humour. In its place, however, is a kind of highly intellectualized wit, a *discordia concors* that has its nearest equivalent in the metaphysical poetry of the seventeenth century. Lowell was not content in his first volume to confine himself to mere finger exercises; on the contrary, the organ-roll is there from the very beginning. When he fails, as in "Christ for Sale," he seems to me to fail completely, but by the same token, his successes, such as "Children of Light," and "In Memory of Arthur

Winslow," are important achievements. In his next volume, *Lord Weary's Castle*, Lowell is to gain a greater control over the violence of his imagination, and at thirty he is to attain the maturity and insight that enabled him to write, as Randall Jarrell has said, one or two poems that will be read as long as men remember English.

JOHN SIMON

Strange Devices on the Banner

There is always joy in certain quarters when a poet starts writing for the theater. In the glorious ages of the drama, from Aeschylus to Goethe and Schiller, drama and poetry lived in wedlock. The nineteenth century broke up that happy union. But sentimentalists like to see marriages last, however unviable they have become, and there seems to be less rejoicing in heaven over a repentant sinner than on earth over reconciled spouses. So, when Robert Lowell's *The Old Glory* was produced off-Broadway, when, in other words, a major American poet was appearing on the stage with verse drama, it was to some—notably to most of the highbrow critics—as if the world has suddenly become a better place.

The Old Glory consists of three one-acters: two shorter ones, *Endecott and the Red Cross* and *My Kinsman, Major Molineux*, based on short stories by Hawthorne, and one longer one, *Benito Cereno*, from Melville's novella. In *Endecott*, a well-meaning Puritan governor of Salem in the 1630s discovers, as he quashes mixed Indian-and-white maypole dancing, that, much as he is against King Charles and the Church of England and their various worldly and opportunistic representatives in the New World, he is not really for the more fanatical aspects of his own Puritans. Yet he is forced into severity against the revelers because "a statesman can either work with merciless efficiency, and leave a desert, / or he can work in a hit and miss fashion / and leave a cess-pool." Endecott opts for the desert, but allows for a little bit of cesspool by way of an oasis.

From *Robert Lowell: A Portrait of the Artist in His Time*, edited by Michael London and Robert Boyers. © 1970 by David Lewis Publisher, Inc.

In *Molineux*, a youth from Deerfield arrives in Boston with his little brother just before Tea Party time. He hopes for a career through his powerful kinsman who commands the redcoats in Boston. During a hallucinatory night in which the Bostonians treat the boys with a mixture of hostility and mockery, the Major is always mysteriously alluded to and strangely unseeable—until the boys have to watch him being killed by the anti-English mob, and are even hypnotically drawn into that mob.

The plot of *Benito Cereno* needs no summary, but it should be noted that Lowell has made considerable changes here (as elsewhere), mostly in the direction of showing the contradictions in the American attitude toward Negroes: "In a civilized country," says Lowell's Captain Delano, "everyone disbelieves in slavery and wants slaves." And the play proceeds to show the rights and wrongs of both blacks and whites.

Clearly, Lowell is trying to capture the ironies, cruelties, and inconclusiveness on which America was built: in *Endecott*, the ambiguities are chiefly religious; in *Molineux*, political; in *Cereno*, racial. Beyond that, though, he is concerned with essential human nature, which he sees as paradoxical, untrustworthy, and, above all, tenebrous. But, regrettably, there are three obstacles he cannot quite negotiate: the limitations of the one-acter, the demands of dramatic form, the problem of stage poetry.

Endecott, for example, is an interesting figure who manages to arouse our sympathetic curiosity, but only at the expense of swallowing up most of the playlet: his psyche exacts much more of our attention than do the perfunctory characters and negligible events of the play. In *Cereno*, attempts at writing some sequences in the manner of Genet, Beckett or Kafka rub uneasily against patches of realism and even a Hollywoodish, shoot-'em-up finale. In *Molineux*, the absurdist mode is fairly consistent (though not so witty as in Beckett or Ionesco), but it clashes with stabs at mythologizing—Charon is introduced as ferryman to Boston, "the City of the Dead"!—and, throughout, one feels a certain confusion between symbol and rigmarole.

Again, dramatizing fiction has required such devices as the confidant, but, in *Molineux*, the presence of the kid brother is not only illogical, it also dissipates the harrowing isolation of Hawthorne's solitary youth. In *Cereno*, Lowell must supply Captain Delano with a sidekick, the naive bosun Perkins, whom the poet intended both as butt of Delano's greater insight and wit and as a Prince Hal, who is supposed to end up, as Lowell put it in an interview, "superior to Delano." This superiority is meant to manifest itself. Lowell tells us, in two short and separate speeches, one of which is only six words long and, allegedly, hinges on Perkins's ironic use of the one word "Sir."

Now this sort of thing is all very well in lyric poetry, but it just does not register in performed drama. And it is true of all three plays that, though they are aware of the things that make a play a play—not merely action and conflict, as commonly held, but also diversified verbal texture, humor, pathos, variety of tempo, absorbing talk, and so on—he is unable either to provide enough of them or to marshal them properly. Thus action tends to bunch up in one place, humor to sound forced, and the language to become static or inconsistent. Babu, for example, far from remaining a slave fresh out of Africa, turns into a Calypso cut-up and connoisseur of American and European history and conditions.

Yet the final problem is the poetry itself. Though written in free verse, *The Old Glory* attains to poetry only in Captain Delano's speech beginning "I see an ocean undulating in long scoops and swells." But this passage is only a slight reworking of Melville's third paragraph; and where it departs from Melville's prose, it improves on it only in one participle, "swallows sabering flies." Here now is a typical passage:

> Things aren't really bad,
> but the time will come, the time will surely come,
> I know the King's mind, or rather the mind of his advisers—
> kings can't be said to have minds.
> The rulers of England will revoke our charter,
> they will send us a royal Governor,
> they will quarter soldiers on us,
> they will impose their system of bishops.

What is the point of printing this as verse? Even its most eloquent champion, Robert Brustein, refers to it in the Introduction as a "prose style." True, there is the precedent of Eliot and Fry, but are *The Cocktail Party* and *Venus Observed* worthy of emulation? Verse that is not really verse can add only pretentiousness to a play, confuse the actors, and throw dust in the ears of the audience. It may even deflect the playwright's attention from his primary task.

But could one not write truly poetic plays today? The answer, apparently, is no. By far the best twentieth-century poet playwright, Bertolt Brecht, kept his poetry off the stage. On it, he allowed for song interludes; otherwise, with trifling exceptions, his plays were in prose. Poetry today has, unfortunately, become a minority art, no longer an integral part of the culture as it was in the heyday of verse drama. Reluctantly, we must accept its divorce from the theater, which must at least *seem* to speak the language of the land. The poet, as writer, may still have a place in the theater; poetry, barring a miracle, does not. What history hath put asunder, no man is likely to join together.

GABRIEL PEARSON

The Middle Years

Lowell's middle poems look informal, easy, natural: poetic forms really do appear to cleave to, and become one with, their statement. The breath's utterances and the poem's artifices grow together in the occasion of the poem's coming into being. It is all as natural as breathing, a spontaneous order, each poem unfolding without strain under its own impulse into its proper shape. But one registers this not simply as an occurrence but an intention. The poems are not innocent: the informality is part of an acknowledged design. The contrast ought to be between closed form and open or projective form, to use Charles Olson's terminology. Projective poetry, or at least its supporting mystique, assumes an open, never occupied space in front of the poem into which it grows and which it defines in the process. The law of its growth is in no wise given by the existence of literature as an institution. The poem is not a product but a process. It seeks the utmost cultural innocence by insisting upon itself as utterance, by riding off into the wilderness upon the unique breathing of the poet.

Here one must risk being contentious. The fiction of projective verse is the counterpart of an ideology whose central concern is to detach American from its European inheritance, a sticky web in which the destiny of the whole continent seems trammeled. One would wish to add that this attempt is itself part of the destiny, one which has helped construct it. The dream of innocence permits technological man to unknow, positively to unwill and so carry on—in deliberate innocence—performing his deed, freed from tra-

From *Contemporary Poetry in America: Essays and Interviews*, edited by Robert Boyers. © 1974 by Robert Boyers.

ditional sanctities and controls. To return poetry to some base in the phys-
iology of the breath is the equivalent of other forms of sanctioning myth—
the myth of the frontier, the myth of economic self-help, the myth of the
westward movement of civilization—that underwrote the exploitation and
devastation of the continent. It is a form of primitivism, resisting the insti-
tutional pressure of literature as a product of history and the repository of
human significance. It substitutes a vision of individual initiatives for the
containing and sustaining vision of a society. Its insistence upon the atomic
valency of the syllable attempts to bypass, by detouring back behind, literary
institutions and precedents, returning language to some state of virginity
before it became dense with societal and institutional import. Literature, let
alone syntax and verse forms, is so much lumber brought in like the rats
with the *Mayflower*, to be put down as quickly as possible. Clearly this view
is absurd: Europe's ghosts groan in the very marrow of the language. But it
retains utility as a mystique that has allowed the wildernesses, internal and
external, to be dared, penetrated and devastated.

History is canvassed as wholesale myth, to be laid flat and folded back
into the landscapes of a perpetual present, as it is in the *Cantos, Paterson, The
Maximus Poems.* The past can always be encountered without guilt, since the
present determines the past, never issues from it. And the present can be
made perpetually anew, in each poem, in each act. Hence the curious in-
nocent cheerfulness, the ontological optimism, the essential refusal of evil
that we find in all these poets, in, most incredibly, the Pound of the *Pisan
Cantos.* Figuratively, however horrific the landscape, the poet is always by
the side of the road to the infectious hospital. He is never encountered on
his way back from it. This is cheering stuff for Europeans, but such poetic
versions of the propaganda of good news they breathe all their lives ought
to be depressing for Americans.

The myth of Adamic innocence is a deliberate obverse of Puritan es-
chatology, but, as an obverse must, issues from the same stamp. How it
connects with objectivism is too tangled a piece of intellectual history to
unravel here. Some parallel gets established between the poem as uncensored
utterance and the poet as unauthored object. In Olson's articulation of Whit-
manian aesthetic, the complex of poet-poem-recipient is to exist innocently,
unprivileged among the objects of the universe. The notion is obviously
consolatory. Each object, unique and self-fathered by the law of its own
development, cannot be held responsible to anything else. As a project the
poem, admittedly lumbered with the common tongue which is as far as
possible molded to local or immediate speech, takes off at right angles from
the joint project of human history. It projects outward into an undetermined

field of infinite space and infinite consciousness. Analogies with journeys, voyages, most pertinently with space exploration, are relevant, as is indeed the quasi-technological jargon that a theorist like Olson employs. The poem, moving ever outward, can never really be called to account in terms of any norm. Indeed, it cannot be criticized, since literature ceases to exist.

The urgency of these issues abounds in Lowell's article on Williams in the *Hudson Review* (1961–62). About Williams himself, Lowell is tender and generous. He praises Williams for his vitality, his grip on environment, even "the shock scramble of the crass and the august." Yet a disciple of Williams must feel that, despite his human community with him, Lowell is utterly out of sympathy, to the point of not being able to engage with Williams's central project. The substitution of reminiscence for discrimination indicates a wariness, a deep withholding. Lowell finally will not endorse Williams's poetics and myths. He is lucid about the implication of that refusal being, in the end, a refusal of America—as "*the* truth and *the* subject." Beneath the hesitant, modest surface of his prose ripples a claim to a more comprehensive sophistication which places Williams and could not, conceivably, be placed by him. In this paragraph praise is subtly subverted by Lowell's sense of his own sense of Williams being more complicated than Williams's sense of himself. The evocation of "Dr. Williams . . . rushing from his practice to his typewriter" is faintly patronizing. There is, too, a syntactical cringing produced by the guilt that troubles sophistication in the presence of innocence:

> The difficulties I found in Williams twenty-five years ago are still difficulties for me. Dr. Williams enters me, but I cannot enter him. Of course, one cannot catch any good writer's voice or breathe his air. But there's something more. It's as if no good poet except Williams had really seen America or heard its language. Or rather he sees and hears what we all see and hear and what is most obvious, but no one else has found this a help or an inspiration. This may come naturally to Dr. Williams from his character, surroundings and occupation. I can see him rushing from his practice to his typewriter, happy that so much of the world has rubbed off on him, maddened by its hurry. Perhaps he has no choice. Anyway, what others have spent lifetimes in building up personal styles to gather what has been snatched up on the run by Dr. Williams? When I say that I cannot enter him, I am almost saying that I cannot enter America. This troubles me. I am not satisfied to let it be. Like others I have picked up

things here and there from Williams, but this only makes me
marvel the more at his unique and searing journey. It is a Dan-
tesque journey, for he loves America excessively, as if it were *the*
truth and *the* subject; his exasperation is also excessive, as if there
were no other hell. His flowers rustle by the super-highways and
pick up all our voices.

The notion of a "Dantesque journey" (Dante being superlatively the exiled
questor for spiritual and evil order) places Williams out of reach of any terms
he would use for himself. Lowell labels, tickets, tames Williams, assimilating
him to an idea of literary tradition whose coercions Williams's poetics is
designed to evade. Yet Lowell, ungenerously at this point, grants all too
willingly that Williams's poems are not artifices, but unpremeditated, natural
occurrences. Hence the speculation that his subject matter "may come nat-
urally to Dr. Williams." While, in that curious rhetorical question that looks
more like an exclamation, Lowell significantly contrasts "the building up of
personal styles" (the poet as architect) with "what has been snatched up on
the run by Dr. Williams," as though Williams were a bank robber or a
swallow. The poems come as easily as roadside or superhighwayside flowers:
they are also—if I catch the right vibration of "rustle," a trifle thin-textured—
victimized and undernourished by their industrial environment. And who
could determine exactly what elaborate circumspection is danced out in the
twice-repeated phrase "pick up"?
      Knowing that Lowell has "picked up things here and there from Wil-
liams," we may suspect that his middle poetry has been loosened and relaxed
by some contamination from the Williams tradition. But the casual address
of the poetry should not deceive us. Each poem is in fact braced by a rigorous
logic. Even where it does not display, it reaches toward a formal rhetoric
that predetermines the poem's shape and destination. Each poem is brought
round unmistakably *by* the poet, whose agency the poem declares, to a
predestined closure. The poem always exists somewhat after some fact, idea,
or event; it is not itself a fact, an idea, or an event. It affirms some order
which is its ground of being. This order may, operationally, be no more
than the conviction that poems should go on being written and that a literature
is still required. Lowell's poems are always bent on being and making lit-
erature. If we remember this, the strategy involved in Lowell's *Imitations*
becomes clearer. Lowell recreates for his own purposes a corpus of poems
belonging to other times and other cultures. He renders them in his own
idiom with a freedom and confidence that raises eyebrows. Equally, however,

he commits his own idiom to the corpus; he adds, offers, sacrifices it, as it were, in order to bring into existence a usable body of literature, as distinct from an eclectic aggregation, from which to derive sanctions, directives, models. The whole operation involves the exercise of a vast tact. Merely to translate would be to become the avatar of foreign cultures. To transform utterly would be to court the solipsism of all imperialisms. Lowell, in his *Imitations*, has both to honor and render alien visions, to domesticate without destroying them. *Imitations* attempts to create a tradition by an individual effort of will, because a literature without a tradition is unthinkable, and because the tradition that filters down through the academies and organs of cultural diffusion is not a possession but so much booty and plunder. To be possessed it must, in the American way, be mastered and retrieved through an individual initiative. Lowell is nowhere more native than in his determination to make Parnassus under his own steam.

For Lowell literature is a precondition for a human world, defined against the circularities and randomness of natural process—a public space in which specifically human purposes declare themselves. Where this space is threatened or extinguished, literature takes over as the repository of its values. The poet may well find himself, even to his own surprise, mounting guard over dead civic virtue. Each poem becomes a defense of literature and behind that of the public order whose disintegrations the poet now registers, but which, in an ideal state, his art exists to celebrate and sustain. Here is the explicit ground of Lowell's career. His poems do not merely perform this function, they reflect and meditate it as well. Indeed, the defensive action for its effectiveness depends upon the poetry being a conscious assumption of this martial role. Lowell confronts in "For the Union Dead" a modern urban devastation in which the civic order is being systematically dismantled. To name is in some sense to tame it. Lowell glares at it, eyeball to eyeball, exposing all his nerves, yet constructing, in the poem's own architecture, an alternative order both to that which destroys and that which is destroyed. The poet substitutes his poem for the statue whose commemorative virtue is no longer acknowledged. The statue once preserved the dead, the past, what had been wrested from the flux of history as destiny. Lowell's poem enacts the death of the statue, its final envelopment by unmeaning. The contained chaos of the aquarium has erupted into and drowned out the public domain: "a savage servility / slides by on grease." To name the horror is to encompass it in the name of a possibility that surpasses it. For the poem is not merely, weakly diagnostic, but militantly braced against the dissolution it utters. The naming is a containment. (Frye would see it as the myth of the hero's struggle with Leviathan.) Lowell redeems the impotent memorial by reinvesting it with the immediacy of flesh and blood, while denying none of its commemorative significance:

> Shaw's father wanted no monument
> except the ditch
> where his son's body was thrown
> and lost with his "niggers."

> The ditch is nearer.

In some sense, Lowell's poem unbuilds the statue in favor of the ditch, the bestial condition of abandonment and loss which the monument traditionally redeems. Characteristically, Lowell's stanza break enacts the ditch which now deepens and widens its significance to take in the gouged soil of violated Boston, the uncommemorated wholesale destruction of the last war ("There are no statues of the last war here") and the last-ditch destructions of atomic warfare. With the utmost economy, almost with elegance, Lowell brings into one focus the commercial greed that has devastated Boston and the Puritan Church that has sponsored the same destructive energies. Its contempt for natural limits, its overweening repudiation of natural death, has, paradoxically, leagued it with the turbulence of a demonic nature. Yet the ensuing atrocity is imaged in the mindless medium of an advertisement. For Lowell to be able to contain and relate both the horror and the mass media's numbing of the horror vindicates the poet's role:

> a commercial photograph
> shows Hiroshima boiling

> over a Mosler Safe, the "Rock of Ages"
> that survived the blast.

Humor plays a liberating part in the effect. It is obscene that a commercial photograph should display the destruction of Hiroshima. But when the sentence carries across the stanza break, "over" (that wildly active preposition) to a Mosler Safe, we are forced into the release of something like laughter at the solemn, self-important, unironic impudence of the commercial imagination. The paradox remains that denials or dishonorings of nature (whether exploitive or theological) give birth not to the super- but the sub-natural:

> the dark downward and vegetating kingdom
> of the fish and reptile.

Hence the ambiguity involved in saying that the safe has "*survived* the blast" (a good poet wrests his meanings from the conceptual substratum of the language itself!). It "survives" only at the expense of life. Yet Lowell does not allow himself easy victories. Obviously, the Mosler Safe is available for every sort of ironic denigration. Lowell simply states; no more. He gives the devil his due. And that ability to rest in statement is in turn an aspect of Lowell's militancy. For it depends upon an ultimate conviction of the efficacy of language, despite all debasements, all dishonorings. Lowell's power of statement points to another use of language, its existence in poems, which unite the world of nature with human intention and meaning. A poem dies; and human nature can assume nature itself as its vesture in its submission to the choice of deaths. Lowell's imagery works incessantly to define, implicitly, the right, the respectful, the decent order which should govern the transactions between man and his world. Thus, "This monument sticks like a fishbone / in the city's throat" asserts it negatively, aggressively. But of Shaw himself: "He has an angry wrenlike vigilance, / a greyhound's gentle tautness." The statuary itself embodies this fusion of nature and artifice: "William James could almost hear the bronze Negroes breathe." Yet in this very line the afflatus of that fusion is chastened by a limiting precision, "almost": artifice and nature are juxtaposed, not confused through agents that relate them: "*bronze* Negroes *breathe*." The peculiar virtue of Lowell's resistance to the endemic and literal dehumanizations of American experience, his refusal to enter America, its vast material growth, slaughter of Indians, enslavement of Negroes, its spoliation of landscape, its exportation of massive violence (all themes treated by Lowell) derives from his realization of complicity in the glamour of those processes, of which his own dealings with madness, vastness, oceanic euphoria, verbal affluence are a part:

> Once my nose crawled like a snail on the glass;
> my hand tingled
> to burst the bubbles
> drifting from the noses of the cowed, compliant fish.
>
> My hand draws back.

The change of tense from past to present is significant. Merely to state a past tense represents in so sensitive a structure as this poem the act of escaping to the past, to childhood, to innocence and evading the small, drab militant virtues of watching and warding in the present. Again, the stanza break enacts the difficulty of the gesture that resists this temptation. The act of resistance means renunciation of fluency and fluidity, a half-unwilling as-

sumption of fixity and dryness. The last line of "Home after Three Months
Away" (the poem which concludes the "Life Studies" sequence) is apposite:
"Cured, I am frizzled, stale and small." To burst the bubble, as the despoilers
of Boston have emptied the aquarium, promises a return to the *plenum*, to
become an open, undetermined, blessedly irresponsible thing, a sheer ut-
terance, like the projectivist poem-object, to reenter the wilderness that
breaks into Edwards's sober couplets:

> the bough
> Cracks with the unpicked apples, and at dawn
> The small-mouth bass breaks water, gorged with spawn.

In "For the Union Dead" Lowell sees himself simultaneously on both sides
of the glass at once, within and without, feeling over its surfaces and seeing
himself as so feeling from the other side: "My nose crawled like a snail on
the glass." The aquarium contains, renders visible, yet resists the demonic
powers of nature which have returned in parody through the rabid growth
of technology: Lowell again "presses" toward them, but this time with the
implication that the medium (and we must consider how far these images of
containments are also descriptions of the poem itself) is cruder, improvised
out of the violence of desperation and yet less effective:

> One morning last March,
> I pressed against the new barbed and galvanized
> fence on Boston Common. Behind their cage,
> yellow dinosaur steamshovels were grunting
> as they cropped up tons of mush and grass
> to gouge their underworld garage.

Whether "underworld" is not too artful, and hence the sign of a nervousness,
is a question. Is Lowell again indulging in premature coercion of his material
into myth? And if so, is this a defense against the destructuring onslaughts
of technological and bestial forces? The whole poem is held rigid and yet
vibrates between the allure of self-abandonment and the restrictions and
tensions of control. Colonel Shaw, Puritan that he was ("he seems to wince
at pleasure, / and suffocate for privacy"), also "waits / for the blessed break"
into the sinister fullness of creation. The "Rem Publicam" of the poem's
Latin motto—object of the poem's creative act—is built on renunciation
("sparse, sincere rebellion"). The Public Thing is a deliberate artifice, some-
thing that stands vertical against all frontal assaults, the lure and corruption
of gravity, the erosion of elements. In the very first line, "The old South
Boston Aquarium stands / . . . now." The poem, too, is to stand, like the
statue, but more, like a piece of architecture. Indeed, architectonic analogies

seem in order. The poem appears to be constructed, sustained by a play of tensions, resistances, contained strains. It is a complex arrangement or investment of spaces. Masses are balanced off against each other. The reader's attention does not enter the poem, nor does the poem envelop or absorb it. We register the various elements of the poem as blocks of discrepant size or weight that still are locked and held in the grip of a fierce compositional energy that ultimately distributes and resolves itself through them. By its last stanza the poem has achieved the demolition of the aquarium and named its destroyer. But it has also put itself in its place. The poem concludes at an intense pitch of what I can only call compositional irony. All the containments and restraints of civilization have collapsed. The monsters are cruising in for the kill. Yet the poem holds, tames them, at the crux of their unleashed aggression. They become compliant to Lowell's vast verbal control: "a savage servility / slides by on grease." The destroyers remain "servile" . . . and one just flirts with the possibility that this servility may be greasy because proletarian; the micks and the wops against Colonel Shaw. But this suggestion merely flickers about the image, and it is one which Lowell would have no difficulty in confronting.

Lowell knows the dangers of the militant, the statuesque, the architectural. Other poems in *For the Union Dead* explore the potential of these virtues for tyranny and petrification. In "Florence" Lowell comes out for the monsters ("tubs of guts . . . slop") against the militant Davids and Judiths, those tyrannicides who exploit and destroy them. He demonstrates how they can become agents of the corruption they should resist:

> On the circles, green statues ride like South American
> liberators above the breeding vegetation—
>
> prongs and spearheads of some equatorial
> backland that will inherit the globe.
>
> > ("July in Washington")

His own bodily architecture is implicated in the subtle poem "The Neo-Classical Urn," which, like the Washington poem, connects with all those Roman allusions, styles, republican monuments which sheathe like thinnest bronze the body politic of America. Lowell, rubbing his skull, recalls by association the turtle shells, themselves prison and armor of the living creatures which he had destroyed by keeping them in a garden urn overlooked by "the caste stone statue of a nymph, / her soaring armpits and her one bare breast, / gray from the rain and graying in the shade," whose classicality is rendered in a faintly Augustan idiom. Again, "Caligula" explores an insanity that tries to turn itself into marble:

> yours the lawlessness
> of something simple that has lost its law.

Finally, in "Buenos Aires" Lowell finds a kind of inverted version of
the military virtues, which have turned totally tyrannical and petrific, the
mirror image almost of the devastation of Boston. Lowell now identifies with
the natural demonic forces—"the bulky, beefy, breathing of the herds." Into
the stony solemnity of the southern capital Lowell dances like a bovine
bacchus:

> Cattle furnished my new clothes;
> my coat of limp, chestnut-colored suede.

In "Buenos Aires / lost in the pampas / and run by the barracks" with
its glum furniture of "neo-classical catafalques . . . a hundred marble god-
desses," Lowell becomes the therapist of so much rigor:

> I found rest
> by cupping a soft palm to each hard breast.

Throughout his work Lowell oscillates between oceanic fluxes of eu-
phoria and horror and a corresponding drive to the security of law, logic,
stability, structure. The flux is outer and inner; often inner and outer are
one and their identification can produce weird puns:

> Now from the train, at dawn
> Leaving Columbus in Ohio, shell
> On shell of our stark culture strikes the sun

which connects, in the same poem, with water, through another "striking"
image:

> On Boston Basin, shells
> *Hit* water by the Union Boat Club Wharf.
> (My italics)

Notice the similar rhyming and syntactical salience of the word "shells."
Queerer is the crude and one hopes unconscious pun that connects "our stark
culture" with one of the ancestors, only a few lines on:

> And General Stark's coarse bas-relief in bronze
> Set on your granite shaft
> In rough Dunbarton.

Lowell's extraordinary feel, tough for texture, weight, density somehow
transfers itself into verbal and syntactical equivalents in the poetry itself as

well as providing much of the imagery. How much, for example, do these lines

> frayed flags
> quilt the graveyards of the Grand Army of the Republic

owe to contrasts of texture and weight? The feel of the stuffs somehow becomes the stuff of the lines so that "Grand Army of the Republic" may look a well-stuffed title, but one which has worn sadly thin. Lowell's poetry returns continually to some somatic base that is Lowell's real presence in the poetry, much more important than any grammatical ego. Here, literally, the poetry is the shadowy but persistent corpus of the man himself, his volatilized and verbally reconstituted self-image. The poem, imaged as a shell, itself oceanic, also represents the tense, elaborate thinness of this own substance, separating the chaos without from the flux within. The process is very self-conscious in "The Neo-Classical Urn."

> Poor head!
> How its skinny shell once hummed.

A Lowell poem, however solid its architecture, never looks other than fragile, friable, only just mastering the pulls and pressures that threaten to disintegrate it. Freud's view of the ego as a hard-won layer of self that achieves enough stability to curb—and yet be fed and thickened by—the importunate, blind drives of the id and that copes and transacts with external reality seems apposite. If Lowell is a post-Freudian poet, this is not primarily because Freud is an inescapable ingredient of secular culture, but because Lowell's poetic practice itself enacts the Freudian drama and is the therapy of the human condition that Freud divined.

Freud was concerned, as therapist, with the making of viable individual existence. He released the fantasies, whose prodigious allure he knew only too well, not to express but to desensitize and reduce them. Lowell's poetic progress could be seen, in similar terms, as a self-therapy. But the terms are too restrictive. One could put it rather that Lowell's poetic career imitates— in an Aristotelian sense—the progress of self-therapy and thereby proposes itself as a case of an ultimately viable existence. It becomes exemplary as a measure of the depth and intensity of the forces that batter the self from within and without, and describes the forms that resistance to these can assume. Lowell as poet becomes the implicit hero of his own poetry, but, of necessity, very much a debunked and debunking hero, diffident, arrogant, self-destructive, perhaps, most of all, despite all, persistent and operative.

It is in some such terms that I would wish to understand the "Life

Studies" sequence. Lowell's treatment suggests not an exhibition but a cauterization of private material and emotion. Interest is not in what is revealed but in what is reserved. These nagging, haunting, futile figures, the threadbare deposits of years of private living, are indeed exhibited, not with contempt or love, but only as they can be contained in poetic architectures—like statues in niches—their features cleansed for presentation, but neither exploited nor degraded nor glamorized. The poker-faced numbness of Lowell's handling of these figures—the balance retained between respect for their integrity and refusal of their domination—is more important than the figures themselves. Our fascination is for how so much emotional dynamite is offloaded and safely defused. Lowell does not permit himself or us any absorption in the depths of memory, emotion, or childhood. We are invited rather to participate in Lowell's craftsmanly concentration on building evanescent emotions and moments and events into solid structures from which they will not evaporate into wistfulness or nostalgia. Lowell hardly permits himself the luxuries of aggression or self-pity or indulges in Hardy-like pangs at pastness. The poetry is designed to keep the past past and the dead dead. If there is any covert emotion it is the quiet grimness of that determination. The success of this cauterization of the past is summed up by the last line of a poem in *For the Union Dead*:

> Pardon them for existing.
> We have stopped watching them. They have stopped
>   watching.

This is the end result of the process initiated in "Life Studies," that phrase that must remind us of the term "still life" and, just as usefully, of its French equivalent *nature morte*. The deliberate deadening of emotion becomes a kind of spiritual exercise, and even achieves a certain perversity in the poem about bringing the dead mother's corpse home, "Sailing Home from Rapallo":

> In the grandiloquent lettering on Mother's coffin,
> *Lowell* had been misspelled *LOVEL*
> The Corpse
> was wrapped like *panetone* in Italian tinfoil.

The sequence shows just the thinness of love in the familiar scene. But Lowell conspicuously abstains from fastening upon the irony of "LOVEL." He simply hovers, brooding glumly, over it, then relinquishes it in the noun-length line "The Corpse." Even the grotesquerie of the last couplet is not allowed to lift into any exuberance. The poem rustles to a dry close on the phrase "Italian tinfoil."

Lowell is really a very nonintimate poet who holds his readers at arm's length, even though much of his reputation and appeal since *Life Studies* depends on his appearing to offer unmediated, secular experience, almost raw. Pleasure in reading him is partly that of recognition, of being shown the artifacts and objects—many of them disheveled, casual, almost nameless—of our common environment. Lowell has a superbly developed sense of milieu, of the tacky and gimcrack surfaces, as well as of the bric-a-brac of our civilization of depersonalized intimacy. How characteristic that the beads that Michael clenches at the end of "Thanksgiving's Over" should be cowhorn and from Dublin. Lowell knows, notices, and with only slightly self-congratulatory hysteria uses such things. But we should notice how far these objects are reapprehended and, as it were, redeemed for attention, by being locked and cemented into larger structures. They are never really innocent, autarchic objects like Williams's red wheelbarrow. They are there because they serve a significance or are at least apt for some design. Thus, in "During Fever" the daughter's "chicken-colored sleeping bag" depends for its color not on the fact that that was the color that it was but on an association with "the healthy country" from which the daughter has returned. While within the drab color scheme of Lowell's recollections in "Memories of West Street and Lepke," Lowell's daughter's "flame-flamingo children's wear" does more than outdo, with that resplendent epithet, the advertiser's euphorics. This is not to deny Lowell's almost uncanny empathy with the furniture of private and mass living, but also to emphasize his simultaneous degree of controlled remoteness from them.

This feel for secular existence finds its counterpart in the casual movement of the poem itself, hardly insisting on its spatial organization, but appearing to unfold without resistance along the line of relaxed reminiscence. For example, "Memories of West Street and Lepke" seems to accrue section by section, without obvious destination, and, trailing off into space, to lapse trickling out into a ruminative silence, which may at any moment revive and grow audible again. The poem seems to hold off from judgement and conclusion. "Ought I to regret my seedtime?" Lowell asks himself, and the poem comes up with no answer, as though it itself were the flower of that seedtime and as such required no confirmation. Anything like a point of view hardly has time to establish itself before it is undercut. Thus, in the first paragraph:

> even the man
> scavenging filth in the back alley trash cans
> has two children, a beach wagon, helpmate,
> and is a "young Republican."

This looks like pretty mainstream irony, but we are not allowed to indulge it for long: in the very next line Lowell adverts to his own parenthood, the creaturely condition which he shares with the scavenger, and wipes the grin at least off his own face. Likewise, the gusty euphoria of the opening lines rapidly reverses within the perspective of his reminiscence:

> Only teaching on Tuesdays, book-worming
> in pajamas fresh from the washer each morning,
> I hog a whole house on Boston's
> "hardly passionate Marlborough Street"

when we are introduced by way of the laundry to

> Czar Lepke
> there piling towels on a rack,
> or dawdling off to his little segregated cell full
> of things forbidden the common man.

which forms a grotesque parallel with Lowell's own situation, hogging a whole house, a thing also forbidden "to the common man." The Lepke situation throws back a retrospective gloom: the poet's own tranquility seems a kind of prison, his routines a prison routine. Like Lepke, he is a prisoner with privileges beyond the common lot. "Hog," of course, connects with Lepke's flabbiness as it does also with "the man / scavenging filth." We become aware of the reek of depression from beneath the rather manic crisp and jaunty production of image and event.

Lowell's right to his mood of euphoria at the beginning of the poem is called into question. It has been bought, apparently, at the expense of a thoroughgoing defensive refusal to make connections. The nine-months-old daughter rising "like the sun" is not the only—and is perhaps only an irrelevantly posthumous—fruit of his "seedtime." There is also the connection, disowned, between Lowell's comparative affluence and "the man / scavenging filth," between his present tranquil—one might say drug-tranquilized—state and the unpriviliged Negro boy with "curlicues of marijuana in his hair" with whom he had once awaited sentence. The question arises for the poet whether he had not been in closer connection all around when in the days of his passionate naiveté he had gone to prison, and whether the manifest violent horror of the decades that produced *Murder Incorporated* was not somehow more hopeful in its openness than "the *tranquilized fifties*."

Is not that tranquility merely a drugged drift toward death, parallel with Lepke's "concentration on the electric chair"?

Flabby, bald, lobotomized,
he drifted in a sheepish calm,
where no agonizing reappraisal
jarred his concentration on the electric chair—
hanging like an oasis in his air
of lost connections.

The poem is a meditation on the edge of middle age. It looks back to a self that is hardly recognizable and—as is to be anticipated on such a theme— forward to death. But the poem also is about the failure to make the middle of a life span connect with and so unify the beginning and the end. The failure is deep and complex: a failure to make the agonizing reappraisal of a state of mind which refuses agonizing reappraisals. The unformed, drifting, apparently randomly wavering lines of the poem is itself an aspect, an expression of this refusal. And yet, despite appearances, this refusal of commitment to a connective structure is turned, against all the odds, itself into a constructive principle. We drift with Lowell's reminiscence as Lepke drifts toward death. And at the moment of the poem's ending, its death, when it runs out upon those eloquent full-stops, we discover the lost connections that Lepke can never find, the analogies and parallelisms and constructive contrasts that have been holding the poem together. The answer to the question is not the poem itself but the alert, militant, and vital chore of unremitting interrogation. The connection in this poem is made through the interrogated fact that everything has come apart and it is made against the defensive grain that would keep it that way. Through this understanding, at the very edge of annihilation, when the poem's sound is about to die away in the air of lost connections, a sense of significance and of coherence is still just able to obtain. So that, after all, the poem survives as a structure which resists the oceanic drift of death of which the mechanical operation of reminiscence is an aspect.

The poem remains an architecture that simulates, anticipates, and thus prevents its own demolition. It is an artfully designed ruin. It only looks like a piece of nature formed haphazardly out of the forces of erosion and accumulation. Secular experience is never, ever, unmediated in Lowell. Not that, in verbal structures, it ever really could be, but, despite appearances, in Lowell's case the ultimate tendency of the poem is to insist upon its structure. Even in this poem, which comes nearer to unmediated existence than any other, in which the poem—the self-substantive, nominative thing— just manages to crystalize out of the stream of poetry—even here there is an appeal to a transcending notion of literature through which this poem takes its place with other poems as part of an order. We are in the presence of a Dejection Ode, of a literary *kind*, and it is that fact which resists the reader's own death-wish; it resists, too, any impulse he might have to drown and be absorbed in the poet's private substance which, until it is owned not as a wholly personal project but as part of a joint human enterprise, must remain part of the chaos out of which order is still to be achieved.

DAVID BROMWICH

Notebook

Notebook marks a point of departure for Robert Lowell—the declaration of
a new form, therefore a new content—just as significant as his earlier shift
in *Life Studies*. The difference, of course, is that *Notebook* is not likely to affect
the mainstream of poetry, because the style it invents is bad—really, because
it is not in any accepted sense a style, but rather the flow of an unremittingly
turbid subconscious. What Dr. Johnson observed of Gray may truly be said
of Lowell in his *Notebook*, that "he was dull in a new way, and that made
many people think him GREAT." The poems do not as a rule work individ-
ually, and so one is proud at having found the patience to wait for a cu-
mulative impression. Still, being in every sense a difficult "case," it is a book
that has to be read; and from a certain point of view, regarded as a necessarily
unsorted testament delivered up from purgatory, it is probably defensible.

It is not opening eyes to propose now, fifty years after *The Waste Land*,
that modern poetry is highly allusive. Yet our awareness extends chiefly to
that quality insofar as it has reference to literature, while modern poetry is
also, and to an extraordinary degree, *privately* allusive. If you want to learn
more about *The Waste Land* you can always look up *The Spanish Tragedy*. But
the private reference is something else again: there aren't any notes, and only
the poet knows his way around the library. A contemporary poet of un-
questionable talent has gone on record as favoring one of his poems over all
the rest because it contained the largest number of private jokes; and the
particular case must appear trivial compared with the tendency. Rare is the

From *Commentary* 52, no. 2 (August 1971). © 1971 by the American Jewish
Committee.

poet who can be as fully comprehended in the reading, without help, as in a public "reading" with its explanations and asides by the author. So, in a way, Lowell has simply drawn this tendency out to its logical end. Resorting to various coded privacies, *Notebook* lies partly submerged, like an iceberg, and its "unrealistic" imagery (the term belongs to Lowell) proceeds by a law of association unknown and unknowable to the reader.

Before entering on a further criticism of the book, it may be well to look at a poem that succeeds on its own. My choice would be "The March":

> Under the too white marmoreal Lincoln Memorial,
> the too tall marmoreal Washington Obelisk,
> gazing into the too long reflecting pool,
> the reddish trees, the withering autumn sky,
> the remorseless, amplified harangues for peace—
> lovely to lock arms, to march absurdly locked
> (unlocking to keep my wet glasses from slipping)
> to see the cigarette match quaking in my fingers,
> then to step off like green Union Army recruits
> for the first Bull Run, sped by photographers,
> the notables, the girls . . . fear, glory, chaos, rout . . .
> our green army staggered out on the miles-long green fields,
> met by the other army, the Martian, the ape, the hero,
> his new-fangled rifle, his green new steel helmet.

After suffering under the strange antics of the other army, the poet offers his bewildered and euphoric toast to the heroes: "Health to those who held, / health to the green steel head . . . to your kind hands / that helped me stagger to my feet, and flee."

What is it that makes all this so attractive? The comical details—the "match quaking in my fingers," the wet glasses—contract the space between author and reader, creating a wonderful sense of nearness; "sped by photographers," with its suggestion of film racing to record the event, is especially clever. Glancing off "For the Union Dead," the echoes of the Civil War sound perfectly balanced and are available to any reader. Most of all, however, the excellence of the poem is in its *persona*: the poet, man of his age, ironic and committed and a bit frightened—this is recognizably the author who wrote: "These are the tranquillized *Fifties*, / and I am forty. Ought I to regret my seedtime? / I was a fire-breathing Catholic C.O." And just this kind of presence is missing in *Notebook* as a whole.

In its place is offered no end of excruciating poses struck by the artist as worn-out neurotic, and the unfortunate point about this is that the poetry hardly ever rises above the squalid world-pain it sets out to relieve. With lines like

> My heart bleeds for the black monster.
> I have seen the Gorgon.
> The erotic terror
> of her helpless, big bosomed body
> lay like slop.
>
> ("Florence")

and with his thunderously indelicate version of *Phaedra*, Lowell once earned consideration as the natural, psychoanalytic heir of Elizabethan violence. Well, but does anyone much want that? If you do not, please beware of *Notebook*, where the author turns out to be more than usually generous with his own peculiar make of gross sexual rhetoric—for example, on the women of George Grosz: "if one could swing the old sow by her tits: / the receding hairline of her nettled cunt / severed like the scalplock by the stroke of a brush." Occasionally a good image working out of the unrealistic technique— "the broken clamshell labelled man"—will eventuate in something awful, and "the clamshell cunted in the ground of being," though capable of para-phrase, is surely beyond redemption. Of the sub-genre known as neurotic poetry Lowell has produced one acknowledged masterpiece, "Skunk Hour"; but he has been lost in the soup ever since. Sometimes he can be very strange and beautiful, as a faithful spirit keeping pulse on the urban blues:

> Nothing more established, pure and lonely,
> than the early Sunday morning in New York—
> the sun on high burning, and most cars dead.
>
> ("Alba")

Depressing materials went to make those lines, and yet their feeling is one of exhilaration. One would only wish for more of this—for a little more respite from sorrow, which unalloyed (and unallayed) cannot help turning tepid, so that the poetry gets contaminated by what it describes.

Much of the book does not fall under that shadow. Much of it is simply chatter, though often of a literary sort; and a certain interest attaches to the observations quoted from other poets—Ransom, Frost, Pound, Bishop, Jar-rell, Eliot—and thereby passed over from chance remark into Immortal Quip. Allen Tate called Lowell's daughter "a Southern belle": you want to re-member that. In effect, the interest taken in such poetry becomes a cover for something else, bearing on voyeurism. The poet is not altogether serious when, after twelve lines of Eliot running on about his relatives ("I've just

found two of mine reviewed by Poe. / He wiped the floor with them . . .
and I was *delighted*."), he throws up his hands and says "Ah Tom, one muse,
one music, had one the luck— / lost in the dark night of the brilliant talkers,
/ humor and honor from the everlasting dross!" Which is horribly predictable
even while it looks tacked on. To show what can happen when the Boswellian
impulse gets mixed in with more important things, let me quote a poem
entitled "Munich 1938," written after the Russian invasion of Czechoslovakia.

> Hitler, Mussolini, Daladier, Chamberlain:
> that historic confrontation of the great—
> firm on one thing, they were against the war;
> each won there, by shoving the war ahead twelve months.
> Is it worse to choke on the vomit of cowardice,
> or blow the world up on a point of honor? . . .
> John Crowe Ransom at Kenyon College, Gambier, Ohio,
> looking at primitive African art on loan:
> gleam-bottomed naked warriors of oiled brown wood,
> makeshift tin straws in their hands for spears;
> far from the bearded, armored, all-profile hoplites
> on the Greek vase; not distant maybe from their gods—
> John saying, "Well, they may not have been good neighbors,
> but they never troubled the rest of the world."
>   August 22, 1968

What is Ransom doing with that African art? Why, exactly, does Prague
put the author in mind of Munich? How does "Kenyon College, Gambier,
Ohio" shed light on the 1938 betrayal and the 1968 invasion of Czechoslo-
vakia? Such are the niggling questions a reader may feel obliged to ask, while
reflecting that "to choke on the vomit of cowardice" is so poor one cannot
quite believe it is Robert Lowell. The three items are being held in juxta-
position, and that's the end of it. Perhaps the hoplites and Russians are
deadly with civilization, as against the defenseless Africans and Czechs.
Perhaps not; and it's no more than a finger exercise—who cares?

On political subjects Lowell does not always seem thus unaccountably
baffled, and I rather like the poem about Stalin, which concludes:

> Stalin? What shot him clawing up the tree of power—
> millions plowed under like the crops they grew,
> his intimates dying like the spider-bridegroom?
> The large stomach could only chew success. What raised him
> was the usual lust to break the icon,
> joke cruelly, seriously, and be himself.

A good illustration, by the way, of . . . the deliberate staging of confrontations with historical characters. With Colonel Shaw, Napoleon, Stalin, this is always in some degree a process of assimilation, and a part of Lowell himself shows up in the lines quoted above. The sequence of poems called "The Powerful" has to be rated the most ambitious effort in the book; and if not entirely successful, it does anyhow want dipping into more than once, as raw matter issuing from the conscience of a bitterly moral historian.

Altogether, I am of two minds about Lowell's *Notebook*. For one thing, there is so much of it—so much good, bad, or just "typical." No one but Robert Lowell would have the temerity to write "Faust's soul-sale," and that, it may be said, is typical. So is "the mammoth mammaries of Aphrodite," or (describing the speaker at a left-wing demonstration) "the audience understood; / anticipating the sentence, they too stood / for the predestined poignance of his murder, / his Machiavellian Utopia of pure nerve." The only name for this is rhetoric, a personal cadence and diction by now (I should say) easily parodied. The quality of the poetry depends—this is obvious— on where the rhetoric is heading. Taking a step downward, it may become rather stupid ("The Republic! But it never was, / except in the sky-ether of Plato's thought, / steam from the ordure of his city state.") or grow astonishingly crude, as when it surveys the corpse of F. O. Matthiessen, "frozen meat." Yet in writing of the death of Randall Jarrell—another suicide, another friend gone by—Lowell suddenly finds the elevation and the evenness of tone which elsewhere in the book he so painfully lacks, and in that single moment he is magnificent:

> you plod out stubbornly,
> as if asleep, Child Randall, as if in chainstep,
> meeting the cars, and approving; a harsh luminosity,
> as you clasp the blank coin at the foot of the tunnel.

An English critic, confronted with *Notebook* and apparently having trouble with it, decided there must be a trick to reading this sort of work. It is much easier if you close your eyes halfway, get settled in a dreamy stupor, and then wait for the meanings to rise up to the surface. I have to admit the novelty of his solution, and having tried it for myself I know that it delivers the goods. But when I ask if this is the way good poetry can be read, the answer must be no. *Notebook* is a special case, perhaps the only one of its kind, lying somewhere between entries in a personal diary and notes toward the making of a real, fully orchestrated series of poems. And it is not hard to tell when an individual poem lies more squarely in the first category or the second; "The Powerful" is plainly nearer the second.

No one is going to read [*Notebook*] with delight, and those who make it their one poetry book of the year (surely Lowell has more readers of this kind than any other poet alive) are going to see even less of the iceberg than they should, unless they are well acquainted with the author's friends, influences, and past work. At all events, there ought to be no two ways about the "crowning achievement" business. It is not that. Fairness will prevail if the book is viewed rather as a transitional step, the worth of which must be determined entirely by future productions. There is certainly no reason to lose heart, since Lowell remains a writer in full possession of an imposing wit, and all his wits.

DWIGHT EDDINS

Poet and State in the Verse of Robert Lowell

With his reticence about his private circumstances, his relative indifference to history, and his advice to poets to avoid "the pressure of reality," Wallace Stevens stands at one end of a modern spectrum. At the other is Robert Lowell—fashioning a drama from his own life, obsessed by a sense and knowledge of the past, and resolved to come to terms with the political realities of his own time in both word and action. Lowell carries on the tradition of Yeats as that tradition was exhibited in "Easter 1916," "Parnell's Funeral," and other poems which found historical human destiny to be immanent in crises of the state, thus making these crises a crucial focus for any poet with aspirations to centrality. This aspect of Lowell's earliest work has been fully recognized; but the labeling of *Life Studies* and succeeding volumes as "confessional" poetry has obscured for many readers the continuity of his focus upon the state, and the complex changes of attitude which form the continuum.

The political landscape of Lowell's first two volumes has been pretty well mapped out by Hugh B. Staples, Jerome Mazzaro, Irving Ehrenpreis, and others. Granted the basically religious orientation which lies at the heart of *Land of Unlikeness* and *Lord Weary's Castle*, it was inevitable that questions of politics should ultimately be subsumed in them by questions of theology— a single-handed reversal, on Lowell's part, of history's movement as reflected much later in *Near the Ocean*, where the New England "theocracy" is shown as having given up its attempt to "command the infinite" and "exchanged

From *Texas Studies in Literature and Language* 15, no. 2 (Summer 1973). © 1973 by the University of Texas Press.

His crucifix, / hardly our sign, for politics" [*Near the Ocean*; all further references to this text will be abbreviated *NO*]. In the early poetry the Rome of "Dea Roma" becomes, as Mazzaro points out, one of the "static measures of man's social framework," from Augustus's attempt at a secular purification to the triumph of the tolerant Constantine which laid the foundation of the "City of God." The seat of world political power and the seat of true Christianity coincide in an ephemeral embodiment of the ideal state, but both secular and religious hegemony decline toward the decisive sundering of church and state in the Europe of the Protestant reformation—a disaster examined in "Charles the Fifth and the Peasant" [*Lord Weary's Castle*; all further references to this text will be abbreviated as *LWC*]. This ironic rendering of Valéry's "César" depicts the leader of the Holy Roman Empire as a pitiful bourgeois simulacrum of the earlier Roman emperor, an inept protector who let the "Ark" of the Church drown in a deluge of Protestantism.

The Protestant state, in the form that it took in Puritan New England, is viewed ambivalently by Lowell. In its intentions to predicate its government of Christian principles, it points back toward the ideal of "Dea Roma"; but in the actualities of its heretical theology, and that theology's natural link with capitalism, it epitomizes all that is most opposed to Christ's teachings. Alienated from what Lowell feels to be the humane tradition of Catholicism, the Pilgrims mercilessly exploited land and Indians under the cover of a twisted conception of themselves as agents of God. Subsequent American history merely changed the targets and the rationale of exploitation; wars fought in the seventeenth century under the banner of religious zeal are fought in the twentieth century under the banner of the capitalistic system.

The victims of the state are seen in "The Holy Innocents" (*LWC*) as "speechless clods and infants" ruled over by the murderous Herod. This kingdom includes all who are caught up in the vast machinery of wars beyond their control, from the hapless Abenaki to the Hungarian workmen of World War II, slaving their lives away in the defense plants of Black Rock, Connecticut, and the civilian bombing casualties of "The Dead in Europe" (*LWC*), begging divine salvation for "us whom the blockbusters marred and buried." Other victims of this machinery, less innocent in Lowell's eyes, are the common soldiers who provide it with fuel. In "Christmas Eve under Hooker's Statue" (*LWC*) the "boyish" Union volunteers "mowed down" at Chancellorsville owe their destruction to Original Sin as embodied in the "blackened Statehouse" of Boston which sent the "butcher" to do its bidding. It is interesting to find this condemnation of the Civil War as yet another political blunder reaffirmed in the revised edition of *Notebook*, where Abraham Lincoln is paired with the empire-crazed Bismarck as one who could seek in war "the continuation of politics." [*Notebook* (New York, 1970); All further citations of *Notebook* are to this revised and expanded edition.] In between these two works, however, Lowell would find this war to be one of the few he could quarry for examples of a moral norm.

In the theocentric universe of the early Lowell, ultimate justice is not only possible, but inevitable; and the state guilty of these innocents' blood is placed, like everything else earthly, in the category of a fallen and transient creation which must face the purification of the Apocalypse. It is this threat—sometimes implied, sometimes explicit—which at once raises the state to the stature of a cosmic opponent and renders it ultimately impotent. Lowell paints the temporal destruction of which political power is capable in horrific colors, fascinated as he is by the violence which he abhors in the name of Christian pacifism; but the destruction is a cause of, and a portent of, the divine retribution which will be visited upon the destroyers at the time of judgment. Thus the head of John the Baptist speaks from a platter of the vengeance to fall upon those who slaughtered him and his people and exploited the land:

> "Surely, this people is but grass,"
> He whispers, "this will pass;
> But Sirs, the trollop dances on your skulls
> And breaks the hollow noddle like an egg
>
> . . . .
>   The Judgment is at hand;
> Only the dead are poorer in this world
> Where State and elders thundered *raca*, hurled
> Anathemas at nature and the land
> That fed the hunter's gashed and green perfection."
>   ("At the Indian Killer's Grave," *LWC*)

The poem "To Peter Taylor . . ." (*LWC*) cites Armageddon as the only effective antidote to war and rampant materialism, when "Whore and Beast and Dragon" appear to put an end to history; and even within history the brutal misuse of political power is answered by holy wrath which is but a portent and symbol of the wrath to come. Certainly this is the case in "Napoleon Crosses the Berezina" (*LWC*). Here the ultimate in secular force and ambition is seen as nothing more than "Charlemagne's stunted shadow," firing his "play-canister" against holy omnipotence as he violates the sanctum of God's law, symbolized by "The Holy Land of Russia." God's vengeance takes the form of a military cataclysm which prefigures the Apocalypse, as the poem's Biblical epigraph makes clear.

Because he is the oracle of this apocalyptic vengeance, the poet of *Lord*

Weary's Castle stands in a special relation to the violent state on the one hand, and its victims on the other. Obviously he shares the sufferings of the latter, since the grinding machinery of the former does not exclude him—a fact dramatized vividly enough by Lowell's World War II imprisonment. But the poet's suffering is tempered by his superior perspective; that is, his religious assurance that the end of history will provide succor for those who believe and will bring brutal justice to those who have stoked the fires of war. In anticipating this justice the poet becomes identified with the divine version of that violence which he condemns in its secular forms, and the reader is faced with the old Christian paradox of the militant, threatening lover of peace.

Lowell's respective relations to oppressor and oppressed actually constitute the stance of the prophet—sympathy and epic lamentation for those upon whom the tribulation falls, antipathy and epic condemnation for those who have brought on this trouble. The resultant tone is hardly a new one in English poetry. The Milton of "On the Late Massacre in Piedmont," the Shelley of *Prometheus Unbound*, the Tennyson of "Tiresias," the Eliot of *The Waste Land*—all of these represent a tradition of the poet as prophet to which Lowell falls heir in his first two volumes. Lowell's critics have, of course, noticed the role: Mazzaro quotes Glauco Cambon's contention that "Lowell speaks like an angry prophet" in his quarrel with history; and Ehrenpreis attacks the role, asserting that "the mere posture of soaring, the air of prophecy, does not make a speech . . . prophetic"; and again, "we cannot help feeling that he enjoys his destructive vision in a way not compatible with his role as prophet, moralist, or recipient of wisdom." The assumptions behind Ehrenpreis's judgments, however, seem specious. A poetic speech that has the "air of prophecy" is "prophetic" in the illusion of art, whether or not it contains invalid predictions or obtrusive rhetoric—a certain amount of this latter appearing, after all, as a standard ingredient in most "prophecies." And to say that the prophet cannot relish his gloomy predictions is to deny the very source of his gift—a momentary and partial identification, as oracle, with God thirsting for vengeance.

This latter point is crucial for an understanding of the relationship between Lowell's style and his unique position with regard to the state in the first two volumes. Because he speaks in a sense for that cosmic force which will finally destroy the state, he must attempt to rise to a proportionate stature in his verse, capturing the violence of rampant sin and the apocalyptic age at the same time that he suggests—paradoxically—an ordering majesty which incorporates this violence into a larger scheme of universal harmony, *sub specie aeternitatis*. Thus, the prophet's visionary experience of chaos existing and to come, and the believer's distress at this chaos, find embodiment in wrenched, violent imagery—so dense that at times it approaches coagulation; while the order which bespeaks the larger scheme is the work of the artist as Creator of his microcosm, where the heterogenous and the shapeless are forced into strict frameworks of meter and rhyme.

It is this penchant for apocalyptic prophecy that gives Lowell his affinity for Jonathan Edwards in "Mr. Edwards and the Spider" and "After the Surprising Conversions" (*LWC*). The link should not surprise anyone who compares an American fundamentalist sermon on damnation with the Catholic sermon in chapter 3 of Joyce's *A Portrait of the Artist as a Young Man*. Edwards's morbidly enthusiastic description of worms and spiders cast into the pit of hell, where "ten trillion" minutes of burning make no dent in time, demonstrates his complete identification with the perspective of eternity. From this vantage point human aspirations shrivel to insect dimensions, and the temporality in which money and power have their sway is dissipated by the prospect of endlessness. It is the prophet speaking, driven to frenzy by the vividness of his terrible foreknowledge; and the same tone, in various modulations, pervades Lowell's first two volumes. The "jellied fire" of "The Dead in Europe" is at once a foretaste and a contributing cause of the divine punishment which is promised, while the states which seem so powerful from an earthly perspective are spiders "in the hands of the great God."

In *Life Studies* Lowell moves downward from eschatology into history— a movement that continues in *For the Union Dead* and *Near the Ocean*. His critics, however, have overestimated the speed and thoroughness of this transition, as regards the poems concerned with matters of state. He abandons the Rome of organized religion in favor of a Paris associated with secular verities in "Beyond the Alps," but he does not immediately abandon his vatic orientation. This retention is demonstrated on one level by the rhetorical cast and the regular prosody and rhyme of the "public" political poems in *Life Studies*, as contrasted with those on Lowell's private life; and the same hold true, with less obvious differentiation, of the poems in the volumes that follow until *Notebook*.

What Lowell does is to modify the prophet mask into the mask of the tragic idealist who sees in the past various norms that he can affirm but none that he can support with fervor as viable possibilities for the present. He retains his high standards of public morality and his attitude of religious commitment even though he has lost the religious framework that provided doctrines of positive action and the hope of justice at the end of history. Now history has no end, unless it is provided artificially by the nuclear holocaust of "Fall 1961" [*For the Union Dead*; all further references to this text will be abbreviated *UD*]—a secular apocalypse that is all the more horrifying for being pointless and that demonstrates Lowell's transitional attitude of "thunder without God" (if I may borrow Yvor Winters's *bon mot* describing fundamentalist religion). The state is no longer a cosmic opponent facing divine judgment; it is "a diver under a glass bell," a bell that also traps the formerly exempt believer as the tons of ocean water bear down in the course of a meaningless naturalistic end to all consciousness.

Nonetheless, such a death is at least touched with some of the grandeur of cataclysm and is thus in keeping with Lowell's modified vatic attitude: negativism on the grand scale, alternating between lamentation and bitter invective over moral situations that are at once intolerable and irremediable. We can recognize here the mask of the heroic satirist, the elevated but bitter perspective of Swift and Juvenal—and it is as a Juvenalian moralist that we may most usefully view the Lowell of the political poems from "Beyond the Alps" to the actual imitation of Juvenal in *Near the Ocean*. In this connection, a stanza that Lowell omitted from "Beyond the Alps" in the *Life Studies* version and later restored becomes highly relevant:

> I thought of Ovid. For in Caesar's eyes
> that tomcat had the Number of the Beast,
> and now where Turkey faces the red east,
> and the twice-stormed Crimean spit, he cries:
> "Rome asked for poets. At her beck and call,
> came Lucan, Tacitus and Juvenal,
> the black republicans who tore the tits
> and bowels of the Mother Wolf to bits—
> Then psychopath and soldier waved the rod
> of empire over Caesar's salvaged bog . . .
> Imperial Tiber, Oh my yellow dog,
> black earth by the black Roman sea, I lie
> with the boy-crazy daughter of the God,
> *il Duce Augusto*. I shall never die."

Speaking himself from the bitterness of political exile, Ovid underscores the irony of the poets' answer to the mother country's request that her culture be nourished by literature. They turn savagely upon her corruption and hypocrisy with merciless satires and exposés, dramatizing not only by their revelations but by their very satirical posture the hopeless fragmentation of art, statesmanship, and military power in a society that would like to claim unity of being. The analogous relation between Lowell and the Washington of his day is obvious enough, in spite of his disingenuous note to *Near the*

Ocean: "How one jumps from Rome to the America of my poems is something of a mystery to me."

Although Lowell's immediately post-Catholic vision is essentially negative, a norm does arise which Mazzaro astutely identifies with Ezra Pound's notion of "past forms of the state"—earlier political crystallizations against which contemporary governments must be measured. In "Beyond the Alps," as most critics have noted, the particular "past form" is furnished by ancient Greece, where government, art, religion, and other aspects of society formed a dynamic, coherent whole. More often, however, Lowell looks back to our own Civil War, to such heroes as his cousin Charles Russell Lowell and Colonel Shaw for a magnificent and complete dedication to the causes of freedom and the health of the republic. Even as late as *Notebook*, we find a tribute to his cousin, and also to an earlier American exemplar, Andrew Jackson, who "stands for the gunnery that widened suffrage." In this more pacifistic volume, however, Lowell is careful to place Jackson away from the realm of modern possibilities, among "Those awful figures of Yankee pre-history" ("Old Hickory").

Despite their Juvenalian overtones, most of the political poems from the period under consideration cannot really be classed as satires; rather they are executed in a heroic-elegiac mode that frequently acquires a mordant satirical edge. The tone is really the result of an organic blending of Lowell's hieratic nostalgia, moral scrupulousness, and "past forms of the state" with ironic diminution of modern pretentiousness and hypocrisy. A fair comparison might be found in the combined effect of the tragic vision that concludes the *Dunciad* and the bitter mock-epical demolitions that precede this vision. "Beyond the Alps" furnishes some vintage examples of Lowell's technique, which relies heavily upon ironic juxtaposition. The sacred mystery of Mary's Assumption, for instance, "glorious as a jungle bird," is mentioned in a context that includes a vulgar crowd yelling "papa" at the Pope, as well as the Pope himself holding an electric razor and a rather inglorious canary. Vatican aspirations to the epical plateau of "the heights once held by Hellas" are effectively punctured by this scene, while the Caesar-like aspirations of Mussolini suffer a similar fate in his description as "skirt-mad" and "one of us / only, pure prose." Diminution of a linguistic sort is achieved by the use of vulgar colloquialisms and puns in connections that would naturally call for dignified language. Thus the Swiss, whose failure to climb Mt. Everest symbolizes the ignoble fragmentation of modern states, are presented as having "thrown the sponge / in once again," while the Pope's loss of spiritual integrity is dramatized by the cheap cleverness of his pun: "The lights of science couldn't hold a candle to Mary risen."

"Inauguration Day: January 1953" (*Life Studies*) and "For the Union Dead" (*UD*) are corollaries of "Beyond the Alps" in both theme and execution. Again, the fragmentation of the modern state is approached as an epical lament edged with satiric irony. Earlier commentators on "Inauguration Day" have noticed the Grant-Eisenhower parallel: two military men whose peacetime presidencies led the country into mediocrity and general decline. They do not, however, seem to have emphasized the heroic criterion of a "past form of the state" which appears in Grant's victory at Cold Harbor and the self-sacrifice of the soldiers who died there for the preservation of "the Republic"—a cherished and once viable ideal. In this context, "the Word," or Logos, is the possibility of valid leadership toward this ideal; but the trust has been betrayed, and the stage is set for the sort of ironic diminution that suggested the betrayals by Pius and Mussolini. Far from being the oracle of the Logos, Grant is its "cyclonic zero," and his sword is "in the groove." Staples objects to the vulgar slanginess of this latter phrase, but this slanginess is functional in its deflating effect, as is the bathos of Eisenhower's nickname in the phrase "the Republic summons Ike." Again, however, rhetorical stylization helps to elevate the final tone of the poem. The verse form is that of a Petrarchan sonnet, and Lowell's imagery acquires the old prophetic ambience as he observes an entire metropolis frozen into stasis, and a mortal vacuity at the Republic's heart.

The heroic norm of "For the Union Dead" is, of course, provided by the sacrifices of Colonel Shaw and his Negro regiment, and the poem has received the careful critical attention that it deserves. I should merely like to emphasize that it is the satirist's eye that contrasts the essential seriousness of Shaw's actions with "civic / sandpiles" of modern frivolity and sees the Massachusetts Statehouse "tingling" and "shaking over the excavations," as it faces a heroic firmness that cows it. Also, there are Swiftian overtones to a vision that finds man servile and ignoble before the triumphant animal kingdom—in this case mechanical creatures of his own creation. A much closer and more telling parallel to the Houyhnhnms, in fact, may be found in "Fourth of July in Maine" (*NO*), where guinea pigs with their "harmonies / of lust and appetite and ease" are depicted as exemplars of a norm that murderous men and their states would do well to imitate: "Evolution's snails, by birth, outrunning man who runs the earth." The pithy, sardonic couplets of this poem—a prevailing form in *Near the Ocean*—enhance the satiric flavor, while diminution and bathos figure in the poem's portrait of the traditional New Englanders: "Emersonian self-reliance, / lethargy of Russian peasants!"

Lowell is obsessed, from *Life Studies* on, with the theme of the decay of republics as evidence of the state's inability to exist for long on an ideal level; and from this obsession come two powerful symbols of political and cultural decay: Latin America and Rome. The most striking use of the former is in "Buenos Aires," retitled "Mania in Buenos Aires 1962" when it was revised for the second edition of *Notebook*. Here the antithesis to freedom, with its ease and exuberance, is provided by a set of images that bespeak the anti-human rigidity and gloom of dictatorship in Peron's Argentina. The intractable "beefy" herds of cattle, the stiff new shoes that cramp the poet's feet, the starched collars, the dough lumps of soldiers on their military chessboard—all of these represent a spirit that nullifies the sacrifice of the "Republican martyrs," in whose graveyard Lowell finds temporary solace as he imagines the stone breast of the Liberty statue becoming a warm and yielding human reality beneath his hand. The nightmare continues in "Caracas I" (*Notebook*), where Lowell describes Venezuela with bitter irony as "This pioneer democracy, built / on foundations, not of rock, but blood as hard as rock." "El Presidente Leoni" is linked with Peron in his fondness for young mistresses, in his indifference to poverty, and in his dependence on sheer military force for survival in the midst of those who hate him: "his small men with 18— / inch repeating pistols, firing 45 bullets a minute, / the two armed guards petrified beside us."

A connection between Latin American conditions and the United States' own decay is made explicit in this poem, when Caracas is described as being "as hideous as Los Angeles, and with as many cars / per head . . . ," and also in "Dropping South: Brazil" (*UD*), when Lowell exclaims "unhappy Americas, *ah tristes tropiques!*" But the most significant and ominous linkage occurs in "July in Washington" (*UD*), where the poet sees "green statues" in the Capitol, riding:

> like South American
> liberators above the breeding vegetation—
> prongs and spearheads of some equatorial
> backland that will inherit the globe.

The Washington of this poem is a polluted, corroding outpost of civilization and republican ideals, which is slowly being reclaimed by the wilderness and its animals, symbols of the savage, barbaric triumph of the "equatorial backland." The corruption pulls into its vortex "the elect, the elected," who arrive with principles of statesmanship that quickly fall prey to the breeding vegetation of compromise and private interest: "they come here bright as dimes, / and die dishevelled and soft." The feeble dream of integrity in government fades as it does in "Mania in Buenos Aires," where Peron's Argentina suddenly seems a portent of the political future: "That day cast a light of the next world."

I shall not treat Lowell's use of Rome here, since it is a standard and fairly obvious symbol of political decline, and since the imitations of Horace and Juvenal in *Near the Ocean* are close to the originals—the latter, in fact, really a translation. It is no doubt safe to say that Lowell is most Juvenalian in his version of "The Vanity of Human Wishes," but is it precisely there, in Juvenal's norm of personal behavior and response, that we find the seeds of a new attitude toward the state on Lowell's part—an attitude that will lead him away from the note of heroic lament and attack toward an almost stoical quietism. In Lowell's version, Juvenal instructs the man who must pray to

> pray for
> a healthy body and a healthy soul,
> a soul that is not terrified by death,
> that thinks long life the least of nature's gifts,
> courage that takes whatever comes.

Juvenal's conclusion is: "I give you simply what you have already." The persona of *Notebook* is not always this stoical, and he never gives up his wish for a longer life; but he varies between extremes of qualified melancholy and qualified joy, and he characteristically gives the impression of a resigned, gently elegiac examiner of historical accounts, including his own. The passivity and the sense of personal impotence in the face of history that Thomas Parkinson finds in *For the Union Dead* are much more pronounced here, but the air of emotional commitment that Parkinson call "panic" has given way to one of poignant acceptance and occasionally of almost neutral observation.

The rhetorical thunder that characterized the prophet mask of Lowell's first two volumes, and that appeared in a diminished, secularized form in the political poems from *Life Studies* to *Near the Ocean*, finds in *Notebook* its antithesis: an almost prosaic cataloguing of the attributes of a subject, accompanied by comments made with studied informality and couched in fragmentary syntax that actually suggests a notebook. The cultivated implication is that the speaker assumes no great degree of control over the chaos he observes. This attitude in turn expands to suggest a lack of control at the cosmic level—which is perhaps why William Meredith referred to *Notebook* as "a propitiatory act to the modern god of chaos." Certainly the obtrusive use of what are meant to seem direct quotations enhances the air of unedited spontaneity. The speaker is wrestling with a tentative ordering that he wishes the reader to consider as possibility rather than inevitable fact, and thus stands at an opposite extreme from the prophet figure whose rhetoric implied an incontrovertible and clearly realized divine plan.

The change of conception is dramatized in the contrast between the Jonathan Edwards of "Mr. Edwards and the Spider" and the one of "Jonathan Edwards in Western Massachusetts," which opens with the picture of a New England where the Puritan theocracy has fallen into ruins. The man whose rhetoric drove church members to fits of terror and even suicide is seen ambling along with notes pinned to his coat to counteract his absentmindedness, and finally as the pastor to "a dozen / Houssatonic Indian children." He has become human and credibly fallible at the expense of the old vatic stature. By the time of *Notebook*, the war on rhetorical poses is so open that Lowell explicitly debunks the histrionic speeches and actions of Robespierre and Louis XVI as mere "theater," equivalent to the aestheticism of Mozart ("Robespierre and Mozart as Stage"), while the hero of "Napoleon" sends his soldiers to death with "grand opera fixed like morphine in their veins."

The Lowell of *Notebook* goes to great pains to dramatize the difficulty of positive commitment and definite decision in modern political affairs. With the possibility of a firm metaphysical anchorage more or less relinquished, he is seized with a strong sense of the moral ambivalence of a given issue or of a particular government that he personally likes or despises; ambivalence is, in fact, one psychological analogue of his style in *Notebook*. Even his sympathy with things Jewish, for instance, is not enough to bring him to decisive alignment in the poem "Israel":

> These sidesteppings and obliquities, unable
> to take the obvious truth on any subject:
> three weeks in the sun of Israel . . . I might have stayed,
> stayed and waited gladly to do service,
> though almost a pacifist, and still not sure
> the Arabs are black . . . no Jew, and thirty years
> too worn.

Not only has he listed four reasons why he cannot commit himself, but two of these are presented with qualification: he is "*almost* a pacifist" and "*still not sure* the Arabs are black." The sonnet's conclusion dramatizes how far Lowell has drifted from his early obedience to a militaristic Jehovah; the thundering commandments have turned into uncommunicating noise in his ears.

In "West Side Sabbath" a conversation between leftist husband and leftist wife reveals a significant ambivalence in their dedication to the cause. He is flippant and she is serious, and the wife herself is torn between two divergent movements of the Left—one a standardized "monochrome Socialism" that insists on "gun-point equality" and the renunciation of privilege; the other the vaguely defined "student-Left," lacking discipline and direction but casual enough to allow room for the little pleasures in life—such as reading the *New York Times*. Irritated by such indecisiveness, Lowell gives way to a moment of envy in "Waterloo" when he looks back to 1815 and asserts:

> You could choose sides then:
> the French uniforms, a blue-black, came out black,
> the British Redcoats gray; those running were French.

By contrast "March I" and "March II," which dramatize the famous demonstrations at the Pentagon, show that the uniform of opposing soldiers can mark gentleness and kindness, in a peculiar combination with the inevitable hostility.

Through these two "Pentagon" poems runs a strong sense of the futility of the demonstration and the ineffectuality of the participants, and this sense is crucial to an understanding of Lowell's new position vis-à-vis the state. The poet is strongly aware of the absurd figure he cuts as he unlocks arms to push his glasses back upon his nose and nurses his "leg- and arch-cramps," while his fellow marchers appear as distinctly unformidable: "mostly white-haired, or bald, or women." The success of the French peasants in storming the Bastille makes the comparison of that prison with the Pentagon cuttingly ironic, while the allusion to "green Union Army recruits" stepping off for "the first Bull Run" recalls one of the North's less successful engagements of the Civil War. This second irony is driven decisively home by the sonnet on Charles Russell Lowell that follows, presenting the image of a commitment that did not boggle at the threat of death itself, much less at the first signs of violence.

The sources of this political futility are depicted by Lowell as partly psychological, rooted in a modern preference for private fantasies over the difficult world of action. In the poem "November 6" Lowell confesses to a fatalistic inactivity on the night of the 1968 elections. Not only is he neglecting to vote, he is not even watching the results on television. Admonished by his idealistic daughter on the telephone, he gives a cynically comic reply and meditates honestly upon his loss of belief that a solution is possible and upon his decadent thirst for the opening of "old wounds" and the "blood-feud" made possible by defeat. Here failure reaches one of the farthest points from idealism, the point where it becomes sadomasochistic. This merciless depth analysis is applied to the pacifist of "Trunks," depicted as a toothless tree-worm writhing in ecstatic and delusory dreams of triumph over those representatives of the state who can easily crush him and his colleagues:

> in the right moment, even the halt-pacifist,
> nursed on straws and wheat-germ, hears the drum-step
> of his kind whistle like geese in converging lines,
> hears the police weep in their fog of Mace,
> while he plants the black flag of anarchy and peace.

Lowell finds historical prototypes for this futile fantasizing in "Coleridge and King Richard." Coleridge has made the unflattering discovery that he is bound to the ineffectual king by "a constant overflow of imagination / proportioned to a dwindling will to act," and Lowell sums up the condition of both by a telling phrase: "white glittering inertia of the iceberg." The sedentary Lowell of Election Night and the dreaming pacifist stare into a mirror that reflects not Colonel Shaw or Sir Thomas More, but a political mutation of J. Alfred Prufrock.

The futility is not, of course, entirely a matter of attitude. There are excellent bases for it in the objective reality of the state's overwhelming power: a reality dramatized by a line from the poem "For Eugene McCarthy," "the state lifts us, we cannot change the state." The ten poems on the Chicago Convention entitled "The Races" demonstrate some of the modes of invulnerability that Lowell sees: raw physical force, naturally, in the use of police and troops; and the masterful corruption of democratic process exhibited in "August," where the Convention appears as "brotherly, stacked, and mean." Another, even more insidious power lies in the obtuseness, as Lowell sees it, of "the great silent majority" who see to it that "the great people can't get elected President" ("Northwest Savage"). Closely related is the sheer weight of custom and tradition that the "Establishment" represents. This is symbolized in "The Pacification of Columbia" by the walls of the great University: "the thickened buildings look like dungeons out / of Raphael, colossal classic, dungeon feudal." The same sense of ponderous authority, not to be denied, shadows the futile protestations of draft resisters from the Lowell of 1943 to a famous pediatrician of 1968 in "The Spock etc. Sentences." Here the authority is mocked, however, by Lowell's choice of a comic symbol for it: "hardrubber bathtub stoppers" in a Boston hotel, which look as though they were ordered for Kings, "then tailored / to the tastes and weight of William Howard Taft."

Frustrated by the near-omnipotence of the modern state, the individual idealist is tempted to join with the like-minded in revolutionary violence; but Lowell rejects this approach as ultimately self-defeating in another Columbia sonnet, "Can a Plucked Bird Live?"

> arms in the hands of the people are criminal,
> arms given the people are always used against the people;
> the only guns that will not kill the owner
> are forged by raised hands . . . fear made wise by anger.

The triumph that this poem sees as the only workable possibility for the humane idealist is a triumph of *attitude*. A sort of passivity has replaced Lowell's early identification with the vengeance of Jehovah and his subsequent identification with the satirist's pen as an agent in the heroic reformation of the state. The individual realizes moral power by psychological victories—by doggedly refusing to offer his approval to bloodshed, on the one hand, or to acquiesce in public corruption on the other. The stakes are a kind of integrity, a constant affirmation of the intrinsically human as against the dehumanizing effects of raw physical duress on whatever scale, and also the favorable judgment of history, hopefully based upon criteria related to this integrity. Lowell dramatizes—and lends impetus to—a model for later historical verdicts when he turns his own attention not only to infamous foreign dictators but certain American presidents and finds them disastrously at odds with his norm of essential humanity.

Hitler and Stalin naturally become ultimate symbols of the antihuman syndrome attendant upon power madness. No less than three poems in *Notebook* are devoted to the Nazis and their leader. One of these, "Attila," equates Hitler with the early barbarian who "never entered a house that wasn't burning" and "could only sleep on horse-back"—both negations of the civilized domesticity that redeems human existence from an animal level. The two barbarians also joined in that larger negation by which everything precious to life was reduced to a pile of garbage. The final villainy lies in becoming the ally of that decay and pointlessness which are, even unaided, the inexorable enemies of everything human. Similarly Stalin, in the poem named for him, is indifferent to the individuality and the organic quality of the state's constituents as he ruthlessly plows them under in his perverse iconoclasm and megalomania.

Shifting his focus to America, Lowell finds the merciless policies embodied in racism and the search for *lebensraum* executed not by Hitler but William Henry Harrison, "selfish little busybody / expelling Indians, legalizing Negroes." Once again the assault upon human integrity and autonomy is symbolized by the dissolution of the organic: "No acid worked more / mechanically on vegetable fibre / than the whites in number." Even Lincoln is related to Stalin by his execution of the Civil War: "politics is the continuation of murder" ("Abraham Lincoln"). Finally another American president, Lyndon Johnson, is almost certainly the target viewed from the stalking horse "Charles V by Titian," a reworking of the poem from *Lord Weary's Castle*. Prosaic and "burgerish," he dreams of spreading democracy while carrying his enemies "with him in a cage." Our Vietnam involvement is the obvious analogue from Lowell's viewpoint, and the parallel of the leaders is greatly strengthened by Charles's political fate: he "gave up office, one of twenty monarchs / Since Saturn to willingly make the grand refusal."

Inevitably, Lowell's rejection of violence as a political *modus operandi* involves his historical survey of power in contradictory situations, where violence seems to have been somehow compatible with the better human traits, including even a superior morality. Alexander, Mohammed, and others receive leniency under these considerations, but one of the most interesting cases in point is provided by the African tribesman of "Munich, 1938," in which Lowell views primitive art in the company of John Crowe Ransom. The statues of native warriors admittedly represent violence in a sense, but a violence limited to their immediate surroundings and day-to-day needs. Their humanity and relative harmlessness are represented respectively by their three-dimensional concreteness and the "makeshift tin straws" that they carry for spears. In contrast the honor-obsessed, imperialistic Greek warriors are seen on a vase as "bearded, armored, all-profile." Like the leaders of Europe in 1938, they consider the keeping of the national word and the acquiring of international hegemony things worth blowing up the world for.

Beyond ambiguity, however, Lowell is able to find relatively uncompromised exemplars of the nonviolent triumph of attitude that he admires, and from their portraits emerges a clear-cut norm of urbane, tempered, and stoically amused humanism. The most outstanding and obvious exponent of this attitude is Sir Thomas More. In the poem that Lowell names for him he appears as fatalistic about what one may expect from the friendship of despots, but nonetheless capable of affirming existence as such and living fully until the inevitable plummeting of his fortunes. His quip at the foot of the scaffold seems to anticipate the Yeatsian ideal of those who come "proud, open-eyed, and laughing to the tomb" ("Vacillation"); but in place of this almost preternatural defiance of death, More's attitude is one of wry, mellow seasoning in the face of superior physical force. In "Lady Anne Boleyn," Lowell explores a strikingly parallel response from another of King

Henry's victims. Faced with the same egomaniacal corruption of power, she preserves her human dignity by refusing to let the horror of death reduce her to quivering bitterness:

> "I hear say I'll
> not die before noon; I am very sorry therefore,
> I thought to be dead by this hour and past my pain."
> Her jailer told her beheading was no pain,
> 'it is so subtle.' 'I have a little neck,'
> she said, and put her hands about it laughing.

Eugene McCarthy's execution was political rather than physical; but in the poem dedicated to him, Lowell admires the same refusal to let go of equilibrium and decency—and also finds a commitment to the quality of life combined with indifference to the claims of vested interests that would ignore this quality:

> Picking a quarrel
> with you is like picking the petals of the daisies—
> the game, the passing crowds, the rapid young
> still brand your hand with sunflecks . . . coldly willing
> to smash the ball past those who bought the park.

For Lowell, this presidential candidate is the modern equivalent of the Crusader King in "Joinville and Louis IX," who refuses to serve the selfish interests of the "bishops, nobles, and Brother of the King" at the cost of deserting "the meaner folk" among enemies.

The gestures of affirmation celebrated above are, of course, the acts of exceptional and isolated individuals; but the possibility of a cultural oligarchy with considerable humanistic influence is raised in the sonnet "Judith." That such an oligarchy is directly related to the problems of political power becomes obvious when we consider the poems "Canterbury" and "Killcrankie," which almost immediately precede the sonnet in question. The earlier "jousting" aristocracies of England and Scotland are shown as neglecting their responsibility to improve their subjects' lives in favor of pursuing the murderous sports of war. In contrast, the New York Jewish "aristocracy" is "airier":

> professors, statesmen, new art, old, the city
> where only Jews can write an English sentence,
> the Jewish mother, half wasp, half anti-wasp,
> says *liberate, literate, liberalize*!

The mother's manifesto may be regarded as the positive plan to which the stoical rectitude of Thomas More and the political idealism of Eugene McCarthy lead, so far as Lowell is concerned. The execution of the former and the electoral failure of the latter are grounds for the poet's characteristic note of despair over the inefficacy of a moral politic; but the other side of the coin is revealed in the contemplation of a spreading enlightenment based upon principles implicit in the lives of these exemplars and others—an enlightenment that may someday make efficacy possible. Lowell's new norm is, of course, open to a wide variety of historical and philosophical objections. But in its chastened assessment of political realities, and of human weakness unsupported by divine strength, it has a more palpable credibility than the triumph of a Catholic world order or the post-Catholic dream of Hellenistic wholeness in "Beyond the Alps."

FRANCES FERGUSON

Appointments with Time: Robert Lowell's Poetry through the Notebooks

When Walt Whitman organized his "Song of Myself" into fifty-two sections in the original 1855 edition of *Leaves of Grass*, that fifty-two-part design was itself a manifestation of Whitman's repeated assertion of the interpenetration between himself—or his selves—and the universe of time progressing through weeks. As a unifying device, this numerology represents one mode of translating the poetic object, with all its presence, into the realm of temporal process and recurrence. The numerology symbolically unifies the poem with the idea of the temporal process out of which it was constituted; but its very obvious factitiousness constitutes an assault on the independent internal unity of the poem. The poem-as-object falls prey to the ravages of process, becomes "subject to revision"—as Whitman himself demonstrated by changing it for the 1860 edition.

Over the last century, the poet's struggle with time has become increasingly conspicuous, if not more intense. A poet like Eliot figures a paradox implicit in the struggle: by pointedly reducing numerous poems to their fragments in order to be able to create his own poem *The Waste Land*, the poet calls into question the historical endurance of the work of other poets and, simultaneously, the endurance of every poem of his own which has come into being before the immediate present. Emerson had earlier, in a journal entry for May 28, 1839, insisted that

> There is no history. There is only biography. The attempt to
> perpetuate, to fix a thought or principle, fails continually. You

From *American Poetry since 1960: Some Critical Perspectives*, edited by Robert B. Shaw. © 1973 by Frances Ferguson. Carcanet Press, 1973.

can only life for yourself; your action is good only whilst it is
alive,—whilst it is in you. The awkward imitation of it by your
child or your disciple is not a repetition of it, is not the same
thing, but another thing. The new individual must work out the
whole problem of science, letters and theology for himself; can
owe his fathers nothing. There is no history; only biography.

The modern poet compounds Emerson's anti-historical subjectivity by dwell-
ing upon the passage of biography—and autobiography—into history. From
the time of Wordsworth, the poem already in print has come increasingly
to seem a tombstone upon the consciousness which constituted it before the
endless wave of Heraclitean flux overwhelmed it.

Poetry must take place in the present, and the modern poet sees that
present as an ellipsis which must be broadened and filled to keep the ever-
encroaching past from colliding with the future. When T. S. Eliot makes
poetry out of self-evaluation in "East Coker" ("That was a way of putting
it—not very satisfactory: / A periphrastic study in a worn-out poetical fash-
ion"), the pastness of his own past words is as onerous as the pastness of the
"worn-out poetical fashion" of previous poets. Since "every moment is a new
and shocking / Valuation of all we have been," new patterns must endlessly
be found if the present is to be seen under the aspect of meaningfulness.

Robert Lowell's career has exemplified in every phase of this perspective
which I have identified as "modern"—the thrust towards ever-more-direct
confrontations with time. Both *Land of Unlikeness* and its impressive sequel,
Lord Weary's Castle, reinvigorate conventional forms while courting a future
of apocalypse. Filtering his vision of contemporary America through the
context of a sordid American tradition, Lowell achieves tremendous power
by an almost total rejection of the present. The apocalypse follows hard
upon the sins of America's past, and the poet treats the time from which he
prophesies as minimal. The violence of language and tone in Lowell's early
poems suggests that the poet-prophet behind them already finds himself
surrounded by the sparks of the "fire next time," after which there will be
no next time.

It seems to me that Lowell very rightly recognized that poems like "Dea
Roma" and "Where the Rainbow Ends" were not susceptible of infinite
proliferation: they very nearly deny themselves the time in which they have
come into being, and they too are charred by the fire which they describe
and invoke. In the early poems, Lowell attempts to outwit time by making
poetry out of the open admission that time has won the contest with human

consciousness. But the poetry is a poetry which can only document its own existence in terms of pyrrhicism.

There may have been silence in heaven after the final prophetic notes of *Land of Unlikeness* and *Lord Weary's Castle*, but the earth had heard such apocalypticism before, without having halted in its course or in its speech. Lowell's heavily allusive language itself pointed the paradox. Although Lowell translated the words of Thoreau, Melville, Jonathan Edwards, the Bible, and a host of others into his own prophecies of the final end, a continuity was implied in the act of translation which produced "The Quaker Graveyard in Nantucket." If Lowell was to continue to write, he had to see his own apocalypse as a temporizing gesture, a beginning rather than an ending.

Although the two earliest volumes of Lowell's poems present themselves as poetry of vision, Lowell substitutes for this a poetics of revision in subsequent work. On the most basic level, even *Lord Weary's Castle* is a revision of *Land of Unlikeness*. A passage from "Cistercians in Germany" (*Land of Unlikeness*) is rewritten to form the ending of "At the Indian Killer's Grave" (*Lord Weary's Castle*); poems like "The Quaker Graveyard in Nantucket" provide *Lord Weary's Castle* an air of completeness which *Land of Unlikeness* lacked. But the varieties of revision embedded within both early volumes come to represent, in the later work, both an embryonic subject and a means for the continuation of the poetic enterprise. When Lowell borrows—or "steals"—from Thoreau, Melville, or Milton in "The Quaker Graveyard," he has already begun to reach beyond the simplest interpretations of Pound's command, "Make it new," and has pointed to a self-conscious treatment of literary works as existing and enduring objects—objects which endure largely through their capacity to change under the pressure of the perceiving consciousness. Just as Eliot's "Animula" and "Marina" simultaneously assert the continued existence of Dante's verses and Shakespeare's *Pericles* and also explore a road not taken by the earlier poets, so Lowell's "The Quaker Graveyard" establishes itself through revision, seeing again.

Imitation—seen as a repetition constituting re-vision—is not Lowell's attempt to supplant all previous literature. Rather, it represents his recognition that poetry documents the movement of consciousness—which can only be living—upon the objects of consciousness—which have an observable existence but no living consciousness. In the eyes of Lowell-as-poet, all previous literature exists initially as an aggregation of enduring objects and, eventually and significantly, as an index to a once-living consciousness which can be renewed by an altering re-vision. If Emerson and Stevens directed their attention to the consciousness acting upon the objects of the world,

Lowell constructs an imaginative order in which the new poem may openly take those very acts of consciousness as objects for a new subjective creation.

What I want to maintain is that Lowell (in *Life Studies*, *Imitations*, and *For the Union Dead*) was adding a complication to the complex dualism from which Emerson insists that

> A man should know himself for a necessary actor. A link was wanted between two craving parts of nature, and he was hurled into being as a bridge over that yawning need, the mediator betwixt two else unmarriageable facts.

For Lowell, poetry becomes a process of engaging the mind of an additional mediator, so that an additional personal and historical time can be recaptured from the other side of inevitable temporal disjunction. Lowell both performs his own mediation between personal time and transcendent time and also introduces the necessity for mediating between his own mediation and the mediations of other consciousnesses. The poet thus becomes both the "mediator betwixt two else unmarriageable facts" and the mediator between two else unmarriageable mediators.

Even in *Life Studies*, the book which has repeatedly been regarded as the poetic autobiography which instituted the contemporary school of "confessional poetry," Lowell was writing a very peculiar sort of confession, because the disjunction between the Robert Lowell writing in the present and the past Robert Lowells which he describes immediately introduces a disjunction between Robert Lowell and other subjectivities external to him. The effort to recapture his own past selves tends to accompany an effort to recapture other past selves.

What initially appear to be the most intensely personal, unborrowed poems in *Life Studies*, poems about Lowell's struggles against madness and the collapse of his first marriage, frequently rely upon complicated movements of the Lowellian speaker into and out of the consciousnesses of various literary characters. "Home after Three Months Away" may serve as an instance of this movement.

> Gone now the baby's nurse,
> a lioness who ruled the roost
> and made the Mother cry.
> She used to tie
> gobbets of porkrind in bowknots of gauze—
> three months they hung like soggy toast
> on our eight foot magnolia tree,

and helped the English sparrows
weather a Boston winter.

Three months, three months!
Is Richard now himself again?
Dimpled with exaltation,
my daughter holds her levee in the tub.
Our noses rub,
each of us pats a stringy lock of hair—
they tell me nothing's gone.
Though I am forty-one,
not forty now, the time I put away
was child's-play. After thirteen weeks
my child still dabs her cheeks
to start me shaving. When
we dress her in her sky-blue corduroy,
she changes to a boy,
and floats my shaving brush
and washcloth in the flush. . . .
Dearest, I cannot loiter here
in lather like a polar bear.

Recuperating, I neither spin nor toil.
Three stories down below,
a choreman tends our coffin's length of soil,
and seven horizontal tulips blow.
Just twelve months ago,
these flowers were pedigreed
imported Dutchmen; now no one need
distinguish them from weed.
Bushed by the late spring snow,
they cannot meet
another year's snowballing enervation.

I keep no rank nor station.
Cured, I am frizzled, stale and small.

Here, Lowell engages poetry to cordon off the time that was wrested from
him by insanity. The talismans left by a now-departed nurse ("gobbets of
porkrind" left for the birds) linger to remind Lowell, who has just returned
from a mental hospital, of the days before he left home, three months before.

And seeing these talismans as physical reminders of lost time, he marks that lost time by repeating "Three months, three months!" before asking with irony, "Is Richard now himself again?" Although this mocking query directly echoes Collie Cibber's adaptation of *Richard III*, Lowell here seems to be casting his returning, though fleeting, identity in the image of Richard II, the poet-king who also bears the marks of a man-poet continually "beside himself," torn between the nothing and the all of his sense of himself. Numbers beat through the poem like notations of broken time—numerical images of the disjointed music in which Richard II images his life.

> How sour sweet music is,
> When time is broke and no proportion kept!
> So is it in the music of men's lives.
> And here have I the daintiness of ear
> To check time broke in a disordered string;
> But for the concord of my state and time
> Had not an ear to hear my true time broke.
> I wasted time, and now doth Time waste me;
> For now hath Time made me his numb'ring clock.

Lowell identifies no coherent selfhood for himself in the poem as he climbs down the chain of being—going from Richard, to polar bear, to dead tulips in his imaging of himself. There is no explicit debate between Lowell's divided selves like that which one recognizes in Richard II—only the abbreviated notation of temporal disjunction in "three months away" echoing from the title. There is no progression in time through the course of the poem—only the consciously exaggerated emphasis upon blocks of time which have evaded Lowell. But Lowell creates an identifiable unity through the complicated allusion to Richard II which dominates the poem. The identification of himself with Richard provides a coherent focus for the absence or multiplicity of selves; it filters the apparently random sequence of images through the memory of Richard's cry, "My thoughts are moments." Lowell's allusiveness here represents an insistence that two disorders (Richard's and his own) make an order, that an order can be salvaged from the surrender to time.

For all its brilliance, Lowell's use of allusion in "Home after Three Months Away" represents a danger. Implicit in the identification with Richard II and in the surrealistic juxtapositions of the poem is a recognition that order must be imported, because the poem takes place so squarely in the present moment that it can find unity only in analogizing itself to images of other disorders. The radical shorthand of Lowell's link between himself and

Richard II stabilizes the poem, but without any sense of limit. The personae of Lowell's autobiographical poems and the images of the poems seem constantly to find no rest within themselves and to point out giddily in all directions toward the external infinite—"no circumference anywhere, / the center everywhere," Lowell everywhere.

In *Notebook 1967–68* (1969) and *Notebook* (1970), the problems inherent in Lowell's allusive techniques have been multiplied, and they have, I think, been met less successfully than in *Life Studies, For the Union Dead*, and *Near the Ocean*. The two editions of *Notebook 1967–68* gesture compulsively toward the world of experience beyond the poems, and *Notebook* compounds the self-conscious inadequacy of these gestures with an additional appeal to temporal process. Although Lowell declares in the "Afterthought" to both volumes that "the time [of the whole volume] is a summer, an autumn, a winter, a spring, another summer" and that his "plot rolls with the seasons," he obviously increases the dependence of his poems on temporal schemata in *Notebook* by adding enough poems to turn each poem into a token of a calendar day. By the time one has read through "The End," one has read 366 poems, one poem for each day of a leap year; and the coda of nine poems similarly refers one to the world of time in the sequence "Half a Century Gone," in which one poem is offered up to each decade of Lowell's life. The coincidence between the numerical patterns of *Notebook* and the year implicitly postulates a kind of unity which enables Lowell to insist that "the poems in this book are written as one poem," but this is a coherence so postulated and so little felt that each individual poem in the volume tends to become indexical. Each poem is less an entity than a reminder of the existence of the others; individual poems—and individual words—undergo devaluation in the notebooks.

From *Life Studies* through *Near the Ocean*, Lowell mitigated his impatience with both words and the world of temporal process with a dogged, exacting scrutiny of specific words and objects. Poems like "My Father's Bedroom" (*Life Studies*), "Jonathan Edwards in Western Massachusetts" and "Hawthorne" (*For the Union Dead*) and "Fourth of July in Maine" (*Near the Ocean*) hang on phrases and physical objects as persistent emblems of the inner minds of the figures about and to whom Lowell writes his verse portrait-letters. He accords both words and objects the dignity of endurance, extending Emerson's observation that "A man may find his words mean more than he thought when he uttered them, and be glad to employ them in a new sense" to give a new sense to the words and objects of other men. In these "middle" volumes, Lowell's language takes on a subdued form of power as his confidence in the inherent freshness of each repeated use of a word appears. Setting the same word down repeatedly, so that the various instances emerge with the force of a new word each time, balances the aggravated insistence upon double meaning in the early work. This linguistic balance points to a heightened, far-ranging conception of *rime riche*, in which word-retentiveness becomes equivalent to the retentiveness of consciousness. Although this poetry recognizes its ability to recapture consciousness lost to time as limited (especially in a poem like "Jonathan Edwards in Western Massachusetts"), Lowell's repetition of his own words and his repetition of the words of others becomes a chant against the erosions of time.

In the notebooks, certain stylistic elements of Lowell's conception of *rime riche* remain. In the third poem of "Harriet," one of the finest sequences in the notebooks, "wood" rhymes itself repeatedly, with a slight difference at each occurrence as the consciousness of the aging process advances itself step by step. The tone of such devices has, however, shifted towards a recklessness which asserts that words and the human consciousness behind them are so fragmented by the temporal process that repetition is no longer incremental. Lowell's notebooks document the movement of a spirit untinged but tarnished by its strain. For all of the labor involved in producing their sheer bulk, they bespeak a passivity, a succumbing to process. Lowell, "learning to live in history," produces a book of poems that is history only by Lowell's interpretation of it—"What you cannot touch." Lines stick in the memory—occasionally even a whole poem here and there, but the fragmentation of perspective has reached such an extreme that the notebooks finally seem to dedicate themselves to the "horrifying mortmain of ephemera."

Each volume of the notebooks is, as Lowell explains, "less an almanac" than the story of his life. Each is his daily life, with dailiness seen in terms of previous Lowell poems, previous poems and prose by other writers, the lives of previous writers, the lives of various historical and literary characters, the future of his daughter, and the future of the world. Although the posited relationship between each poem and the course of a year lodges the poems firmly in the present, the present also has to bear the weight of infinite time. In the poetry from *Life Studies* through *Near the Ocean*, Lowell depended upon the organizing powers of memory to rescue vanishing emblems; in the notebooks, he rushes to change before those emblems can have been admitted even as "sad, / slight useless things to calm the mad" ("Waking Early Sunday Morning," *Near the Ocean*). The poetry of the notebooks is a poetry of restlessness. And Lowell casts his restlessness into justification and example in poems like "The Nihilist as Hero," the first poem in the sequence "We Do What We Are."

One wants words meat-hooked from the living steer,
but the cold flame of tinfoil licks the metal log,
the beautifully unchanging fire of childhood
betraying a monotony of vision.
Life by definition breeds on change,
each season we scrap new cars and wars and women.
Sometimes when I am ill or delicate,
the pinched flame of my match turns living green
the cornstalk in green tails and seeded tassel. . . .
A nihilist has to live in the world as is,
gazing the impossible summit to rubble.

Image-making—and the imagination itself—burst through the bland
pessimism of the bulk of the poem as the "pinched flame" is transfigured
into a "living green / the cornstalk in green tails and seeded tassel." But
Lowell allows himself only this two-line moment of insight before annihi-
lating it with a doctrinal pronouncement. In the earlier version of this poem,
Lowell concluded with the ambiguity of

> Only a nihilist desires the world
> to be as it is, or much more passable.

By allowing the poetic consciousness the possibility of discovering the "more
passable" as the more tolerable for even a moment, the ambiguity of these
lines validates the image-making which precedes them. In the later version
of the poem, however, Lowell closes the poem by reduction in announcing
the dictates of the "world as is" to his poetic self. However strong the
imagination may appear in its Joshuan capacity to tumble "the impossible
summit," "rubble" seems a paltry product—a fallen Babel rather than a
Jericho won. As in the poem, "For John Berryman," with its crashing, self-
reflexive punning on "working through words" (". . . you / know what I
have worked through—these are words. . . .), Lowell denies both his words
and his images any but the briefest possible duration. There is no ending to
this kind of poetic process, because it passes time by endless cancellations
of every new moment. The re-vision represented in the notebooks disdains
the orders which can be constructed from a new penetration of the objects
of memory; and although the poetry is occasional, it rests upon a fundamental
impatience with the occasional. Re-vision, here, is the recognition that the
moment which Lowell has just admitted into the present has already passed
away, so that Lowell can only look back over his shoulder at his rejections
as he moves towards the future.

Perhaps the most disputed boundary in poetry and criticism from the time of Pound and Eliot to the present is the line between change and chaos. Poetry—like that of Lowell's notebooks—which takes for subject the temporal "world as is" continually seeks that uncharted line and tries to walk it. But a demon guards that line from too-near-approach; and the demon is always the monotony of change—the dullness of chaos—which infects a poem like "The Nihilist as Hero." In the midst of the ceaseless change in Lowell's notebooks, a future must endlessly be postulated, a future in which all will be made well—and given significance. "Reading Myself," the final poem in the sequence "We Do What We Are," is perhaps the most explicit of Lowell's manifestos of this dedication to the future. Summarizing his previous poetic career, Lowell derisively describes himself:

> I memorized tricks to set the river on fire,
> somehow never wrote something to go back to.

However impossible it may be to step twice in the same river, to step a second time in a river of fire is unimaginable, and Lowell sees himself as having burned his rivers along with his bridges. The poem breaks off, shifts to describe a poetry which treats its own lack of finality as a mark of promise:

> No honeycomb is built without a bee,
> adding circle to circle, cell to cell,
> the wax and honey of a mausoleum—
> this round dome proves its maker is alive,
> the corpse of such insect lives preserved in honey,
> prays that the perishable work live long
> enough for the sweet-tooth bear to desecrate—
> this open book . . . my open coffin.

Instead of the rubble of "The Nihilist as Hero," Lowell extracts building materials in "Reading Myself." The "wax flowers" of continually satisfying, contained poems past change are converted into their essence, the wax and honey of a mausoleum never complete as long as the poet remains a continuing subjectivity. Lowell's distrust of his own past poetical moments—which is, for the most part, a radical distrust throughout the notebooks—persists in "Reading Myself," but the one poem which will include all of his poems hangs over the imagery as an emblem of future, transcendent justification.

The scarcity of Lowell's appeals—implicit or otherwise—to any sort of justification in the notebooks yields a poetry which has already provoked numerous critics to *pro forma* complaints about the obscurity of modern poetry in general and Lowell's notebooks in particular. Lowell certainly seems to court obscurity in choosing his poetic materials: "I have taken from many books, used the throwaway conversational inspirations of my friends, and much more that I idly spoke to myself." Although one imagines that most poets find their materials in much the same way (as Wordsworth was certainly doing in poems like "We Are Seven"), Lowell's description of his borrowing from literature and life is notable for its insistence upon the obliquity of his materials. The stuff of his poetry in the notebooks, we are told, is necessarily obscure, because Lowell is continually writing from a process of intense and random personalization.

The degree to which Lowell adheres to the personalization of his ma-terials—the degree to which Lowell shuns the universalization and stabili-zation of his materials—becomes striking when one contrasts a poem like Randall Jarrell's "Well Water" with almost any of Lowell's sonnets in the notebooks. Jarrell opens his poem with a "throwaway conversational inspi-ration" that announces itself as such ("What a girl called 'the dailiness of life' "). In Jarrell's treatment, however, that "throwaway" inspiration has to be reasoned through, explicated, and cast into images. " 'The dailiness of life' "

> is well water
> Pumped from an old well at the bottom of the world.
> The pump you pump the water from is rusty
> And hard to move and absurd, a squirrel-wheel
> A sick squirrel turns slowly, through the sunny
> Inexorable hours. And yet sometimes
> The wheel turns of its own weight, the rusty
> Pump pumps over your cold sweating face the clear
> Water, cold, so cold! you cup your hands
> And gulp from them the dailiness of life.

The monotonous repetition of the *petit quotidian* transforms itself in the last four and a half lines into the repetitiveness of a psalm-singer. Although the images of the poem move from pump-handle through squirrel-wheel with an obvious nonchalance about the laws of the physical universe, "Well Water" finds a point of rest beyond its own randomness and illogicality. For the poem concludes with the kind of benevolent pragmatism which allows one a moment of naive shamelessness in which to suggest hopefully that even randomness and pain may have saving, unfathomable purposiveness.

Jarrell's "Well Water" is a useful contrast to most of the poems in Lowell's notebooks, because is uses a "throwaway conversational inspiration" to drive a wedge into the sense of oppressive temporality. However strong

Jarrell's distrust of words may have been at other moments (as in "*Seele im Raum*," for example), he here appropriates the random phrase and allows the mind's retentiveness to become a process of extension which generates its own opposite—redemption. The disjunctive incrementalism of the poem— the movement from "the dailiness of life" to well water, to pump, to squirrel- wheel, to pump turning of its own weight—plays a curious confidence trick upon time, the antagonist to the consciousness. "Well Water" is a modern definition poem which bases itself on the assumption that every definition, symbol, or analogy invariably constitutes a failed identity, because time exercises a continually disjunctive pressure, diverting the subject from its object and the self from its anterior self. By taking the monotony of temporal change for subject and by worrying that temporal monotony through a necessarily failed process of definition, Jarrell manages to cancel time alto- gether—so that the human consciousness appears to stand free of the tem- poral process altogether.

Whereas Jarrell's poem converts a throwaway phrase into an attempt to isolate a moment beyond the temporal process, Lowell continually uses the throwaway to move toward a vision of temporal reductivism. The extreme personalization of the poetry in the notebooks necessarily involves obscurity, because Lowell insists upon melting the recognizable rocks of the grounds of knowledge into ephemera. In the sequence, "Writers," for example, Lowell denies himself all access to both the work of other writers and to the enduring consciousnesses which emerge from that work. Consequently, he adopts something like the stance of a literary gossip, recounting his conversational exchanges with various writers. The written word lasts too long, Lowell seems to be saying; and his writers become talkers, being granted only their unenduring and least essential vocabularies.

In these poems, Lowell's writers talk with him in a tone ranging from triviality to incoherence; unprotected by the order of their art, they stand exposed, muddled. But most terribly, the death-rattle creeps into their voices, as in "Robert Frost," the final poem in the sequence "Writers."

> Robert Frost at midnight, the audience gone
> to vapor, the great act laid on the shelf in mothballs,
> his voice musical, raw and raw—he writes in the flyleaf:
> "Robert Lowell from Robert Frost, his friend in the art."
> "Sometimes I feel too full of myself," I say.
> And he, misunderstanding, "When I am low,
> I stray away. My son wasn't your kind. The night
> we told him Merrill Moore would come to treat him,

he said, 'I'll kill him first.' One of my daughters thought
   things,
knew every male she met was out to make her;
the way she dresses, she couldn't make a whorehouse."
And I, "Sometimes I'm so happy I can't stand myself."
And he, "When I am too full of joy, I think
how little good my health did anyone near me."

The figure of the vulnerable Frost is tremendously moving, but his
interlocutor Lowell is distressing. The Lowell writing the poem recalls an
earlier Lowell of youthful ebullience and callowness, but both Lowells tend
to bully Frost—the later Lowell being more successful. Frost's defense
against the earlier Lowell was his own ominous pronouncement upon the
painful distance between one's work and one's life, the self and others; but
the later Lowell takes Frost at his word—and with a vengeance. The poem
catches Frost in the middle of the process of divesting himself of all the props
of his art; and the art is all prop, so that Frost's poetical self seems to exist
merely as a mask for the audience. Like the audience, the poetical self
vanishes. Additionally, the opening phrase—"Robert Frost at midnight"—
hangs over the whole poem to locate a temporal endpoint past which there
can be no appeal to any saving aspects of process. The play on Coleridge's
title thrusts Frost against a Faustian moment of decision while also reducing
him to the unconscious, ephemeral existence of an insubstantial natural ele-
ment. As a part of process, Frost must move or be moved, but that movement
is limited by his moment; past midnight, there is only annihilation.

The conversational inspiration emerging through the poem is obscure,
no because one needs to know Frost's or Lowell's history in order to com-
prehend the poem. Although one may puzzle over the mention of Merrill
Moore, the poet-psychiatrist, the fundamental obscurity of the poem lies in
its reductive appetite for rushing its subject out of existence. Randall Jarrell,
in a comment on Lowell's poetry, maintained that Lowell "bullied" his early
work but that "his own vulnerable humanity" had later been "forced in on
him." In the notebooks, however, Lowell often appears to bully vulnerable
humanity—in himself and in others. Having recognized the inevitability of
temporal process and its culmination in mortality, Lowell becomes the hench-
man of time as he pushes the characters and objects of his poems from the
obscurity of meaninglessness into nonexistence.

Lowell's obscurity in the notebooks is the obscurity of a poetry which
set out, through a poetical recasting of a traditional Hegelian view of historical
time, to make nonbeing increasingly tangible with the passage of historically

poeticized time. In Hegelizing his poetry, Lowell attempts to yoke the pas-
sage of personal historical time with a growth analogous to the development
of the phases of World-History, as Hegel outlines them in his preface to *The
Philosophy of History*. For Hegel, the culmination of the development of World-
History is the Old Age of the German world:

> The Old Age of Maturity is weakness; but that of Spirit is its
> perfect maturity and strength, in which it returns to unity with
> itself, but in its fully developed character as Spirit.

For Lowell, the culmination of the development of personal history is
the Old Age of "Obit," the final poem in the notebooks:

> Before the final coming to rest, comes the rest
> of all transcendence in a mode of being, stopping
> all becoming. I'm for and with myself in my otherness,
> in the eternal return of earth's fairer children.

In spite of Lowell's echoes of Hegel, however, one wonders whether the
notebooks actually figure forth the development which "Obit" proclaims.
Through the poeticized personal history of the notebooks, Lowell clearly
struggles to reconcile a language of representation—which represents the
world of historical time—with a language of self-consciousness or spirit—
which represents the eternity beyond duration. Poetry is his mode of con-
fronting historical time, but poems are not properly objects of historical
change, because literary works are (in some sense) intended to endure. In
subjecting his poems to historical time by linking them to temporal schemata
and by discarding them in progress, Lowell incorporates his own words, his
own poems into a language of representation which marks duration. Although
some such incorporation seems inevitable in any poetry striving for self-
consciousness, Lowell's minimalization treats everything under the rubric
of representation and historical time as mere rubble to be stared through.
"This History, too . . . is for the most part, really unhistorical, for it is only
the repetition of the same majestic ruin." Lowell frequently and finally stakes
the poetry of the notebooks on the possibility of wresting a spiritual autonomy
from the flux of historical time. But one finishes each of the volumes, *Notebook
1967–68* and *Notebook*, with a sense of the triviality of historical time and a
Satanist's question—Can there be an eternity which is not in love with the
productions of time?

STEPHEN YENSER

Imitations

(Let us speak of the osmosis of persons)
—EZRA POUND, Canto 29

the dissolution of ourselves into others, like a wedding party approaching a window.

—"The Landlord"

The opening paragraph of the introduction to *Imitations* includes these pointed statements:

> This book is partly self-sufficient and separate from its sources, and should be first read as a sequence, one voice running through many personalities, contrasts and repetitions. I have hoped somehow for a whole. . . . The dark and against the grain stand out, but there are other modifying strands.

If one were not acquainted with Lowell's habit of constructing whole books of poems, as distinct from collecting poems and placing them between two covers, these claims might seem enigmatic or pretentious. It is certain that in spite of these remarks, many reviewers and critics have regarded *Imitations* as a collection of more or less free translations that bear little relationship to one another. Ben Belitt, himself a translator and poet and one of Lowell's most competent critics, is typical in this respect. After declaring that the first sentence quoted above is a "startling expectation" for a poet-translator to have, Belitt simply disregards it and proceeds to discuss (quite percep-

From *Circle to Circle: The Poetry of Robert Lowell*. © 1975 by the Regents of the University of California. University of California Press, 1975.

tively) several individual imitations. Frequently, even the claim about the independence of individual poems is not taken quite seriously, and perhaps partly for this reason *Imitations* has not had the undivided critical attention that most of Lowell's other volumes have received.

At least two recent critics, however, have paid heed to Lowell's plea that the book be considered "a whole." In a review of *Near the Ocean*, Daniel Hoffman has described *Imitations* as "a long, fragmented poem of the self, struggling in its engagements with history." As Lowell struggles with the poets whom he imitates, "with their vision, their style, their problems, they become his doppelgängers in their times and he theirs in our time." Basing his own discussion upon Lowell's comments and Hoffman's translation of them, Richard J. Fein has cataloged and discussed several of the themes— including war, infinity, the quest, and nature—that recur through this volume. Fein's discussion concerns itself with texture rather than structure, however, and not even his sensitive reading discloses the intricacy of the interrelationships among the imitations. . . , for *Imitations* is a work of such dimensions that it warrants a small book. . . .

Lowell's *Imitations* have been brilliantly chosen and scrupulously arranged. The organization of this book resembles that of *Lord Weary's Castle* in that emphases are placed upon the beginning, middle, and concluding poems; in both cases, by repeating key words and images at these points, Lowell calls attention to the generally symmetrical structure of the books. But if in the placing of emphases by means of motif *Imitations* recalls *Lord Weary's Castle*, the extent of the use of motif reminds us of *Life Studies*. The title of this volume itself indicates its relationship to its predecessor, for in addition to its literary meaning, *imitation* has a pertinent musical denotation. According to the *Harvard Brief Dictionary of Music*, imitation is "the restatement in close succession of a musical idea (theme, subject, motive, or figure) in different voice parts of a contrapuntal texture," and it "may involve certain modifications of the musical idea, e.g., inversion, augmentation, dimunition, etc." From the concept of modified "restatement" of materials to that of "different voice parts," this definition is parallel to Lowell's talk of "modifying strands" and of "one voice running through many personalities, contrasts and repetitions."

The organization of *Imitations* is thus more closely related to that of *Life Studies* than to that of *Lord Weary's Castle*, but it is probably most closely related to that of the book that succeeds this one in Lowell's canon. As the brief comparison with *Lord Weary's Castle* has suggested, *Imitations* has a basically symmetrical structure in which the central section is the crux; and . . . the profile of *For the Union Dead* is remarkably similar. Moreover, within the symmetrical framework of each book, there is a series of interrelated groups of poems which function in the manner of a narrative.

One can distinguish two principles upon which the narrative of *Imitations* rests, the most important of which corresponds to the development of character in a more conventional narrative and the other of which corresponds to the development of action or plot. The first of these principles, which is the one upon which Lowell's introduction focuses, provides for the changes in the outlook of a persona who, depending upon one's immediate point of view, either undergoes or emerges from the experiences reported in these poems; for if it is true that there are "many personalities" in this volume, it is also true that there is but this "one voice." Lowell's two phrases, which seem contradictory at first glance, can be reconciled easily enough by means of a simple but unorthodox distinction. This distinction is between the two terms, often considered synonymous, *poet-speaker* and *persona*. For present purposes, the former term refers to the speaking figure in any single poem, while the latter designates the figure who is capable of speaking in all of these voices. The poet-speaker in a given poem, then, although not identical with the persona, is one facet of the latter, or one of the instances from which we infer his development. The other instances include all of the other poet-speakers and a few of the more properly dramatic figures, such as Achilles in the imitation of Homer, who seem to be projections of the persona. If the persona is not identical with any of the poet-speakers or dramatic figures, neither is it identical with the poet, since the poet is the creator of this collective mask just as he is the imitator of the individual masks. Lowell's "many personalities" are the points that comprise the curve of his "one voice."

Perhaps the mixture in that last metaphor indicates the advisability of positing a second principle upon which this poetic narrative operates. The course of the persona's experience is frequently best described in terms of spatial metaphors, and one reason for this is that there is something like a plot in *Imitations*. This principle is harder to analyze than the first because it is both less consistently and more variously invoked. Since thought and feeling rather than deed and event are the concerns of the lyric, action is as necessarily intermittent as character is unavoidably present in this volume; and since lyric themes are fewer than the settings that they involve, action at this most rudimentary level is bound to be more diverse than the "personalities" in *Imitations*. Nevertheless, there are enough references to similar events to constitute a sketchy plot, and this plot is demonstrably of the epic variety. These poems were selected and arranged with an eye to the events and the settings which they involve, and their events and settings are often those one would expect to encounter in a heroic poem—battles, shipwrecks, descents to hell, and the like. *Imitations* opens with Achilles at Troy, and its next to last stanza concerns Leonidas at Thermopylae. But the clearest instance of the use of such a plot is in the central section, which is the nadir of the persona's development, the dark night of the soul, and in which the most important poems describe voyages and shipwrecks. If Ovid, whose *Metamorphoses* is the source of the drawing on the title page, provides the model for the changing personalities in this book, then Homer, whose *Iliad* is the source of the first poem, is the guiding spirit for its ghost of a plot.

To catch these two principles at their point of intersection, one might say that *Imitations* presents the metamorphosis of Achilles, the type of the warrior, into Odysseus, the type of the voyager. Such a description, however, would still be limited, not only because many of the poems are not concerned with wars or voyages, but also because even the combination of the two heroic figures would only be symbolic of the fundamental subject of the book. Another type that might be singled out as representative of this subject, and which would be more comprehensive than either of the heroic figures because it would conceivably include them, is that of the poet. Almost as many of these imitation are concerned with poets and writing as are concerned with wars and voyages; moreover, as E. R. Curtius has pointed out, there is a seemingly inherent connection between composing poetry and voyaging, and the "boat of the mind" was a commonplace in antiquity. Indeed, just to mention the metaphor is to call to mind a host of poems in English much older than Pound's *Cantos*, Crane's "Voyages," and Stevens's "Prologues to What Is Possible," as well as several of those imitated in this volume, including Baudelaire's "Voyage" and Rimbaud's "Bateau ivre." Lowell's volume is another of these symbolic voyages, but it is to be distinguished from most other such symbols in that what it signifies (the life of the poet) is virtually identical with what it is (a series of closely related, many-voiced poems). *Imitations* is a particularly apt synecdoche for the poet's life because the poet, be he Homer or Ovid or Lowell, undergoes in the course of his work those changes of personality which Lowell insists are at the heart of this book.

Because it is an intricately organized whole with the requisite beginning, middle, and end, it seems that the volume must remain a symbol for the poet's life rather than a reflection of any particular life. The persona, it will be remembered, is not necessarily Robert Lowell. At the same time, as we shall see, the structure of *Imitations* is not such as to preclude its being a reflection of Lowell's own life as well as a symbol of the life of the poet.

With these general observations in the background, it is possible to examine the structure of *Imitations* in more detail. Although any such analysis must ignore some of the more subtle transitions between poems and the quite natural deviations from the overriding scheme, *Imitations* can be divided into seven sections. The ordering of these sections constitutes both a symmetrical arrangement, in which poems and short sequences approximately equidistant from the center counterbalance one another, and a progressive structure, in which a spiritual descent turns into an ascent and an affirmative conclusion grows out of a nihilistic beginning. On several occasions, Lowell goes out of his way to indicate some of the more salient points of this scheme, and it is mildly surprising that almost no one has yet taken his hints. The earliest of these indications, and the one which has been admirably glossed, appears in the first line of the first poem, "The Killing of Lykaon," which is based on two separate passages from the *Iliad*. In Lowell's translation, Homer's line becomes "Sing for me, Muse, the mania of Achilles." The remarkable aspect of this line is that the Greek word which corresponds to Lowell's "mania" is "ménin," which means "enduring anger" or "divine wrath" and is invariably rendered as such by Homer's translators. While the Greek word is cognate with "mania" and Lowell is therefore more "literal" in a peculiar sense than other translators, the denotations of the two words in their respective languages are significantly different. Lowell's choice, then, enables him to declare in the opening line of the volume his imitative license. That it has an even more important function might be suggested by quotation of another line, this time from one of the poems at the center of the book. In Rimbaud's "Les poètes des sept ans" there is the line "Vertige, écroulements, déroutes et pitié," which in Lowell's version becomes "dizziness, mania, revulsions, pity." Since neither "écroulements ("ruins" or "failings") nor "déroutes" ("routs" or "confusions") would ordinarily be rendered with "mania," one might suspect a connection of some sort between this line and the one in "The Killing of Lykaon." Nonetheless, it is likely that the suspicion would be dismissed if one were not to notice that Lowell makes a similar alteration in translating the last line of Rilke's "Die Tauben" in the poem that ends the book. In the course of transfiguring Rilke's entire last stanza, Lowell turns the last line into "miraculously multiplied by its mania to return." Especially since this imitation has been conspicuously displaced from the chronological order that obtains almost everywhere else, it is clear that Lowell intends "to return" us to the volume's initial line; and once this connection of end and beginning has been noticed, it is likely that we will pay more attention to the line in the Rimbaud poem in the middle of the book.

Simply by placing the word "mania" in these critical positions, Lowell outlines the general curve of *Imitations*, or designates three of the seven sections noted above: the introductory poem, the central sequence, and the concluding poem. Comparable devices are used to designate other groups of poems and the relationships among them. Just after the imitation of Homer and just before the imitation of Rilke, there are short sequences (selections from Sappho and Der Wilde Alexander, on the one end, and from Annensky and Pasternak, on the other) which serve as transitions between these poems and the core of the volume; and Lowell points up the parallelism of these sequences (our second and sixth sections) by making them reflect on another. The concluding lines of the third poem based on Sappho and some lines near the end of "Hamlet in Russia, A Soliloquy," based on several poems by Pasternak, stand in such a relationship. Lowell's version of Sappho runs:

> The moon slides west,
> it is midnight,
> the time is gone—
> I lie alone!

The poem derived from Pasternak recalls the preceding lines with this image:

> The sequence of scenes was well thought out;
> the last bow is in the cards, or the stars—
> but I am alone, and there is none.

Both passages deal with the solitariness of the speaker, both address themselves to a darkness not only of the night, and both stress the passing of time. The chief difference between them is that "The sequence of scenes," which is to say the majority of these imitations, has passed. The significance of this distinction, which involves a discussion of the progressive or incremental structure of the volume, is the subject of a later inquiry. At this point, it is necessary to touch upon some of the other indications of our tentative division of this "sequence of scenes."

The transitional sections under consideration reflect one another by means of several other anticipations and echoes, the most important of which concern a symbolic forest. In "Children," the forest is a mysteriously dangerous place, " 'alive with snakes,' " which must be avoided if one is not to be lost. As the herdsman admonished the children:

> "Well then, get out of the woods!
> If you don't hurry away quickly,
> I'll tell you what will happen—
> if you don't leave the forest
> behind you by daylight,
> you'll lose yourselves;
> your pleasure will end in bawling."

The children, however, did not leave the woods, and the poem intimates that they did indeed lose themselves:

> Where we picked up violets
> on lucky days,
> you can now see cattle gadding about.

In a note in *The Penguin Book of German Verse*, whose prose translation Lowell seems to have consulted, the editor remarks that "this poem is probably an allegory." Like the lyric itself, this note is probably disingenuous, since the former is certainly allegorical; but the specific subject is sufficiently ambiguous to justify editorial reticence, and it is this ambiguity which Lowell exploits later by means of oblique allusions. When we find, near the end of the book, one poem in which the speaker enters the woods and is advised by them, and several poems set in the forest, and one poem entitled "In the Woods," we must suspect that the persona was one of the children who never got "out of the woods" and that Lowell is bending the allegory to his own purposes. The suspicion is enforced and more specifically directed by the reference to the woods as a place where one must suffer strange transformations, where " 'you'll lose yourselves,' " a reference that is recalled by the last stanza of "The Landlord," another imitation of Pasternak:

> as if life were only an instant, of course,
> the dissolution of ourselves into others,
> like a wedding party approaching a window.

This loss of the self repeats but radically revises the notion as it is allegorized in "Children." . . . "The Landlord" and "Children" parallel one another by virtue of both position and subject and thus help to establish the ordonnance of the *Imitations*.

The titles of several key poems exemplify most simply this structural use of parallelism. The beginning of what might be called the third section of *Imitations*, for example, is marked by an imitation of Villon's "Le grand testament," a title that is translated by Lowell's "The Great Testament." Lowell's title, apparently unremarkable, assumes some importance when it is realized, first, that the adjective "grand," while often interpolated, was not originally in Villon's title and, second, that its inclusion and translation as "Great" suggests more immediately a relationship between this poem and an imitation of Montale called "Little Testament." Since it occurs late in this volume, at the end of the Montale poems, and since it and the poems just preceding provide a thematic response to "The Great Testament" and the poems succeeding it, "Little Testament" concludes our fifth section.

Similarly, if more dramatically, Lowell translates Hugo's "A Théophile

Gautier" as "At Gautier's Grave" and then alters the title of Mallarmé's
"Toast funébre" to "At Gautier's Grave" too. The clear implication is that
these poems are to be paired, and this implication is strengthened by the
positions of the two poems: on either side of the long selections of poems
from Baudelaire and Rimbaud. Just as the two "testaments" seem to begin
a third section and conclude a fifth, so the two poems on Gautier seem to
conclude the third and begin the fifth.

Between the two poems on Gautier, there are twenty-six poems based
on Baudelaire and Rimbaud. Since the number of imitations of Baudelaire
(fourteen) is the largest of any author, while the number of imitations of
Rimbaud (twelve) is second, and since these two are the ninth and tenth of
eighteen authors, there is no doubt that what we will call the fourth section
is the heart of this volume. Throughout this section there are so many
repetitions of phrase and image that it is difficult not to regard them as
allusions intended to lace these two sets of imitations together. Of course it
might be coincidental that the first Baudelaire poem opens with the indict-
ment that "we spoonfeed our adorable remorse, / like whores and beggars
nourishing their lice," while the last Rimbaud poem is "The Lice-Hunters";
and that in the one poem the devil sat by the sickbeds and "hissed," while
in the other "the royal sisters" sat there and "hissed"; and that the tone of
the first poem, which occurs before the spiritual crisis discussed below, is
summarized in the phrase "yawning for the guillotine," while that of the
second, which follows this book's dark night, is epitomized by the phrase
"begged the fairies for his life"; and so on through the other poems. But
even if these echoes are considered accidental, the whole question of whether
they are so could not have suggested itself without a recognition of such
definite structural indicators as have been noted. From one point of view,
Imitations is a dense reticulation of internal allusions; and once this self-
allusive quality has been noticed, the problem is not so much in showing
how the allusions create a structure as in keeping that structure from seeming
to fade into the texture of allusions.

The symmetry of that structure, however, might not be as sharply
limned as it might appear from the preceding adumbration. The *Imitations*
fall almost as easily into five or nine sections as into seven; and once the
principle of balanced arrangement has been discerned, it might even be
advisable to dispense with references to sections altogether. Nevertheless,
the outline sketched above does have the merit of providing a framework for
a discussion of the narrative or progressive aspect of that structure.

DAVID KALSTONE

The Uses of History

"Unerring Muse who makes the casual perfect": this is Robert Lowell's tribute to Elizabeth Bishop in a recent poem. There is a lot to be learned from Lowell's admiration for a poet whose work is so entirely different from his own. In interviews, in public statements, he has often seemed full of yearning, ready to change his spots, to move toward the offhand, the un-amplified statement. He remembers giving readings on the West Coast in March 1957: "I was still reading my old New Criticism religious symbolic poems, many published during the war," the poems which appeared in *Land of Unlikeness* and *Lord Weary's Castle.*

> I was in San Francisco, the era and setting of Allen Ginsberg, and all about very modest poets were waking up prophets. I became sorely aware of how few poems I had written, and that these few had been finished at the latest three or four years earlier. Their style seemed distant, symbol-ridden and willfully difficult. . . . I felt my old poems hid what they were really about, and many times offered a stiff, humorless and even impenetrable surface. I am no convert to the "beats." I know well too that the best poems are not necessarily poems that read aloud. . . . Still, my own poems seemed like prehistoric monsters dragged down into the bog and death by their ponderous armor. I was reciting what I no longer felt. What influenced me more than San Francisco and reading aloud was that for some time I had been writing

From *Five Temperaments.* © 1977 by David Kalstone. Oxford University Press, 1977.

prose. I felt that the best style for poetry was none of the many
poetic styles in English, but something like the prose of Chekhov
or Flaubert.

The book that emerged from these frustrations, *Life Studies* (1959), was ex-
plicitly autobiographical, growing out of Lowell's attempts to write a prose
memoir (and indeed including a prose fragment in the first edition). Its final
poem, "Skunk Hour," was dedicated to Elizabeth Bishop "because re-reading
her suggested a way of breaking through the shell of my old manner."
    The poems in *Life Studies* do not sound like either Bishop or the Beats.
If anything, their manner resembles that style of "scrupulous meanness"
which Joyce chose for *Dubliners*—terse, unblinking, declarative and free of
narrative comment. Bishop's work had reminded Lowell in "the qualities
and abundance of its descriptive language . . . of the Russian novel." There
is not much of that descriptive generosity in *Life Studies*. But there is, in
poems which touch on "the woe in marriage," mental illness and the frosty
eccentricities of New England family life, the conviction that prose plainness
must be his model—not because of Pound's dictum that all poetry should
be at least as well written as prose, but rather from the compulsive belief
that prose is "less cut off from life than poetry is." Lowell speaks of the
"ponderous armor" of his early poems, of the "shell" of his old manner, of
his tendency to fall into a "mechanical, gristly, alliterative style that does
not charm much, unless . . . I try to change my spots."
    Over the years the pressure toward and yearning for authenticity have
been expressed with progressive intensity. Critics have come to see Lowell's
enterprise almost entirely in those terms: "a long struggle to remove the
mask, to make his speaker unequivocally himself." Lowell's own self-
descriptions encourage that view, but always wistfully, as if some yet greater
immediacy were possible. He came to see *Life Studies* as catching "real mem-
ories in a fairly gentle style." He had intended—and later felt it as a limi-
tation—that each poem in that book "might seem as open and single-surfaced
as a photograph." With *Notebook*, the poem he published and republished in
two successive revisions over five years (1967–73), the object was more pro-
visional: no "stills" as in *Life Studies*, but rather "the instant, sometimes
changing to the lost. A flash of haiku to lighten the distant." "If I saw
something one day, I wrote it that day, or the next, or the next. Things I
felt or saw, or read were drift in the whirlpool, the squeeze of the sonnet
and the loose ravel of blank verse." A tone of gratitude and relief crosses
Lowell's comments on the casual: "Accident threw up subjects, and the plot
swallowed them—famished for human chances."

Yet only three years after the revised *Notebook* appeared, in a publishing
flourish no less-established poet could venture, most of the same poems,
revised, with eighty or so new sonnets added, reappeared as *History*. "All
the poems have been changed, some heavily. I have plotted. My old title,
Notebook, was more accurate than I wished, i.e. the composition was jumbled.
I hope this jumble or jungle is cleared—that I have cut the waste marble
from the figure." That Lowell should use the analogy of finished sculpture
for *History*, that something as tentative as *Notebook* should grow into a larger,
more resonant statement—everything implied by the title *History*—reveals
one of Lowell's authentic temptations. He has been rewriting his poems from
the very start, one book remaking poems from another. But *History* is the
most ambitious of these ventures, the latest example of his desire to "make
the casual perfect." We are in the presence of a continuing, baffling, often
invigorating struggle in his work.

I

It is easy to portray Lowell's career as one of dramatic change: *Life
Studies* marking a conversion to the urgent, the day-to-day, biography and
autobiography. Lowell himself saw the book as a passage out of a period
when "most good American poetry was a symbol hanging on a hatrack."
But *Life Studies* presents only one aspect of a career which has changed
directions several times and whose appetites are complicated and contradic-
tory. From the very start Lowell had been drawn to autobiographical poems
of the sort that he wrote with more ease and success in *Life Studies* and *For
the Union Dead*. The Winslows, his mother's family, enter his poetry as early
as *Land of Unlikeness*, his Cummington Press book of 1944, and *Lord Weary's
Castle* (1946), his first commercially published volume. There are lines specific
and prosy enough to pass for later work: "Her Irish maids could never spoon
out mush / Or orange-juice enough"; "Belle, the cat that used to rat / About
my father's books, is dead." The story of how Lowell struck his father when
he interfered in one of the young man's college love affairs was first told in
Lord Weary's Castle, retold in the revision of *Notebook* and again in *History*,
each time beginning in practically the same way: "There was rebellion,
Father, and the door was slammed."

Lowell's eagerness to incorporate autobiographical experience into his
poems is not confined to an early, middle or late stage of his career. But it
does have its seasons. He was to say after *Life Studies*: "I don't think that a
personal history can go on forever, unless you're Walt Whitman and have a
way with you. I feel I've done enough personal poetry. . . . I feel I haven't

gotten down all my experience, or perhaps even the most important part, but I've said all I really have much inspiration to say, and more would just dilute. So that you need something more impersonal."

We needn't take that statement as implying a simple boundary between public and private, though at least one critic, Patrick Cosgrave, is able to write confidently about *The Public Poetry of Robert Lowell*. Lowell "burns," according to Cosgrave, "to judge men and affairs against an immutable and objective standard." *History* replaces *Notebook*, it is true. But Lowell doesn't move between public and private with the authority and ease of a Horace or a Pope. We are dealing with a troubled and prodigal poetic personality whose returns from private anxiety to draw a public breath are accompanied by overexposure and a certain conspicuous waste. Historical judgment and public distance—the tone realized, for example, in "For the Union Dead"— are entangled with his own partly victimized awareness that he is a Lowell and a New Englander. He is, as Richard Poirier put it, "entrapped . . . among evidences of a past that promise but will not yield their secrets." It is in that sense that Poirier sees Lowell as "our truest historian." In his best poetry there is an unspoken and often intended plot: the ambition to write resonant public poetry is corroded again and again by private nightmare, by a failure to escape ghosts of the past. "The past, none of which he can reject or scarcely forget, exerts a control on his imagination, and his imagination, even while working to discover new and liberating possibilities in itself, can only be kept sane by reaching some understanding with the past."

Lowell said that at the time he wrote *Life Studies* he didn't know whether it was a death-rope or a lifeline. His handling of autobiographical material since then suggests that he is still not ready—and perhaps need never be— to answer that question. The tone of *Life Studies*, flat and unadorned, was indeed a breakthrough. But his changes of manner since then, his likening *Life Studies* to still photographs, suggests that those poems did not solve the problem of authenticity, of a style adequate to the facts of his biography or his poetic ambitions. *Life Studies* poses questions about personal poetry and provides only one kind of answer, a solution to which Lowell did not remain committed. . . . Our problem with *Life Studies* is to identify the continuing drama behind the poetry's apparent lack of insistence, its apparently documentary surface. For Lowell, plain autobiography is an impulse, not an answer.

Perhaps the best way to frame a reading of *Life Studies* is to take examples from poems written before and since its publication. Among Lowell's earliest and latest works, though not his best, are attempts to deal with the moment when, as a young man, he struck his father. (This is an incident he does not touch in *Life Studies*, his first overtly autobiographical book.) There are three published versions. The first, "Rebellion," appears early in his career, in *Lord Weary's Castle*. Twenty years later, a significantly changed version appears in the "Charles River" sequence of *Notebook*, and again, only slightly revised, as "Father" in *History*.

All three versions are gnarled and go off in strange directions. But the first, "Rebellion," is *clearly* evasive. It veils most of its narrative in transferred action ("You damned my arm" rather than "me").

> There was rebellion, father, when the mock
> French windows slammed and you hove backward, rammed
> Into your heirlooms, screens, a glass-cased clock,
> The highboy quaking to its toes. You damned
> My arm that cast your house upon your head
> And broke the chimney flintlock on your skull.

The *History* version keeps some of the evasiveness and transferred nervousness ("the highboy quaking to its toes"), but also opens to bluntness: "My Father . . . / I haven't lost heart to say I *knocked you down*." What is most noticeable in versions twenty years apart is the pressure in both cases to make the poem *signify*. Like many of the poems in *Lord Weary's Castle*, "Rebellion" sees human action on an apocalyptic scale. "Cast your house upon your head" bears an almost biblical weight as well as the force of the young Lowell's anger against his New England Puritan and mercantile forebears. We know the mood from the poem which precedes "Rebellion" in *Lord Weary's Castle*, "Children of Light": "Our fathers wrung their bread from stocks and stones / And fenced their gardens with the Redman's bones. . . . They planted here the Serpent's seeds of light." Lowell stands aside, the avenging angel, in such bitter poems directed against tough old Yankee capitalism.

In "Rebellion" he tries to understand a moment of drama between father and son as part of that larger drama, an opportunity for the satirist's savage indignation against "the world that spreads in pain." The young man dreams that the dead catch at his knees and fall. And then

> Behemoth and Leviathan
> Devoured our mighty merchants. None could arm
> Or put to sea. O father, on my farm
> I added field to field
> And I have sealed
> An everlasting pact

> With Dives to contract
> The world that spreads in pain;
> But the world spread
> When the clubbed flintlock broke my father's brain.

The confusion of tenses at the end of the poem ("I have sealed . . . But the world spread . . .") suggests awakened doubts, his willingness to look again at the incident and see the whole poem as a way of evading a primal rage. There is a shift, if a veiled one, to take responsibility, to admit membership in the world he so busily denounced: "But the world spread / When the clubbed flintlock broke my father's brain."

Twenty years later the poem is revised to be part of a drama of "witheredness"—to use a word Lowell applies to other later poems. In *History* he uses several sonnets to take an expansive look at the college love affair which provoked his assault on his father. The context is now provided by poems in which he presents himself as an aging father, haunted by the ghosts of his own parents, as in "Returning":

> If, Mother and Daddy, you were to visit us
> still seeing you as beings, you'd not be welcome,
> as you sat here groping the scars of the house,
> spangling reminiscence with reproach.

In "Father" the inescapable Oedipal tale fades into a tableau from a hushed procession of fathers, as Lowell himself takes his father's place.

> I have breathed the seclusion of the life-tight den,
> card laid on card until the pack is used,
> old Helios turning the houseplants to blondes,
> moondust blowing in the prowling eye—
> a parental sentence on each step misplaced. . . .
> You were further from Death than I am now—

"Devoted to surrealism," as Lowell claims to be in *Notebook*, successive revisions turn the original "glass-cased clock" into a less and less palpable furnishing. In *Notebook*, it is a "sun-disk clock," but *History*, "you heirloom clock, the phases of the moon," as if to make the object itself transparent and through the figures of its decorated face to slip into the astrological certainty of the event. Images of exhaustion and process ("old Helios turning the houseplants to blondes") make parenthood seem to invite rebellion. With the end of the poem, Lowell abruptly shifts directions, and with no syntactical link, introduces a final mockery. The burned-out houseplants imagined as "blondes" lead to a sexual defiance from across the generation gap, delivered by

> that Student ageless in her green cloud of hash,
> her bed a mattress half a foot off floor . . .
> As far from us as her young breasts will stretch.

The momentary passing or "feel" of the incident becomes much less important to Lowell than the act of placing it in an elegiac context, a vein very congenial to him. The poem also allows him a half-ironic, half-yearning look at contemporary youth. My point is that entwined with the autobiographical impulse is a corresponding rhetorical effort to amplify events, to see them as part of the patterns of his past. In *History*, as in *Lord Weary's Castle*—but with far more humanity in the later version—Lowell refuses to trust a provisional account of this incident. We are not dealing, as some of his prefaces invite us to believe, with "the instant, sometimes changing to the lost."

I am concerned, then, with the varying autobiographical modes Lowell has devised throughout his career. Something in him resists the casual "I" of autobiography. Often, in his most interesting poems, counter-currents draw him away from any mere *present* he is trying to inhabit. In a poem like "Rebellion," and more successfully in "Children of Light," he tends to identify his personal anger with protests against hypocritical and prosperous New England Puritanism, as if satire could dispose of or resolve the quarrel with his personal past. The Catholicism he adopted at that time, as many critics have pointed out, was a peculiarly Calvinistic one, a platform from which he could denounce Boston and the mercantile life he made it stand for; all histories, personal and public, were instances of the Fall. Many of the poems of *Lord Weary's Castle* allow him to hold the past at a distance, as Boston hangs in the pans of judgment in "Where the Rainbow Ends." In the early poems he identifies himself with the finality of apocalyptic religious energy, as if this distancing were the only means he had to breathe and survive. This is a poetry of resonant judgments and memorable closing lines: "The blue kingfisher dives on you in fire"; "The Lord survives the rainbow of His will."

The force with which the younger Lowell saw the world and the past destroyed—poem after poem performed this gesture—was a reflex of their hold on him. No poetic mode was to be congenial unless he could, as Irvin Ehrenpreis puts it, "not only . . . treat himself as part of history but . . . treat history as part of himself." How was he to incorporate what Ehrenpreis calls "the tone of fascinated disgust" (with society) into poems where, as at the close of "Rebellion," he begins to acknowledge his own nature, to feel himself alive and part of the world he denounces? How was he to find a voice which did not conceal his driven nature, his private grief and resentment, behind his social and religious stances? Was there an acceptable tone in which a poem might suggest historical judgments, but still reveal itself as the crazed glass of private vision? It was from this dilemma that Lowell describes himself emerging, with his "life studies" and especially with "Skunk Hour," which he called "the anchor poem in the sequence."

II

"Skunk Hour" was written in August and September 1957, after the California reading trip in which Lowell began to feel that his old poems "hid what they were really about." His account of writing the poem shows him at a crossroads. He wrote it backwards; the last two stanzas were, in point of composition, finished first, then the two preceding stanzas. The admissions of mental breakdown ("My mind's not right") were on paper relatively early. But in its completed version, the poem opens with four satirical stanzas, introducing a decayed Maine village, which balance the four more "personal" stanzas Lowell had first composed.

He has performed a characteristic maneuver. The opening description, as Lowell put it, "gave my poem an earth to stand on, and space to breathe." It also allowed him, as the poem was written, to withdraw from psychological intensity into what seems at first glance to be wry social comment. "I found the bleak personal violence repellent. All was too close, though watching the lovers was not mine, but from an anecdote about Walt Whitman in his old age. I began to feel that real poetry came, not from fierce confessions, but from something almost meaningless but imagined."

In "Skunk Hour" Lowell was willing to forego the savage withdrawn irony of *Lord Weary's Castle* for a "more or less amiable picture." "Sterility howls through the scenery, but I try to give a tone of tolerance, humor, and randomness to the sad prospect. The composition drifts, its direction sinks out of sight into the casual, chancy arrangements of nature and decay." Lowell seems aware that he *needs* this Maine landscape, but not as a platform of insulated moral judgment, the kind that separates the speaker from his world in angry poems like "Children of Light." Nor is it simply that a decaying Maine village offers a setting appropriately pathetic for the troubled "I" who enters undisguised in the fifth stanza. Looking at this landscape proves to be a challenge for the speaker. The satiric stanzas, at once smug and melancholy, are charged with his characteristic fears, later exposed and acknowledged. John Berryman was right in saying that "the poet is afraid of outliving himself," and that the opening stanzas glance apprehensively at figures who have gone away and at survivors who endure for nothing more than dotage and empty marriage.

Through the casual tones of the opening play a tune and rhythms which we later come to identify as the diseased speaker's own obsessive sounds: monosyllables with final and emphatic rhymes. "I myself am *hell*." "I hear / my *ill*-spirit sob in each blood *cell*." "The *hill's skull*." Cars that lie together "*hull* to *hull*." Syllables like that have from the start been beating insistently through the poem.

> Nautilus Island's hermit
> heiress *still* lives through winter in her Spartan cottage;
> her sheep *still* graze above the sea.
>
> . . . .
>
> she buys up *all*
> the eyesores facing her shore,
> and lets them *fall*.
>
> The season's *ill*—
> we've lost our summer *mill*ionaire,
> who seemed to leap from an L. L. Bean
> catalogue. His nine-knot *yawl*
> was auctioned off to lobstermen.
> A red fox stain covers Blue *Hill*.

It is only at the fifth stanza that veils drop away and the dull inescapable toll is recognized for what it is. What we took for muted satire may or may not be objectively true; we come to see those opening stanzas tinged by the speaker's diseased vision as the poem goes on in the same throbbing sounds to reveal his disabilities.

> One dark night,
> my Tudor Ford climbed the hill's skull;
> I watched for love-cars. Lights turned down,
> they lay together, hull to hull,
> where the graveyard shelves on the town. . . .
> My mind's not right.
>
> A car radio bleats,
> "Love, O careless Love. . . ." I hear
> my ill-spirit sob in each blood cell,

as if my hand were at its throat. . . .
I myself am hell;
nobody's here—

only skunks, that search
in the moonlight for a bite to eat.
They march on their soles up Main Street:
white stripes, moonstruck eyes' red fire
under the chalk-dry and spar spire
of the Trinitarian Church.

I stand on top
Of our back steps and breathe the rich air—
a mother skunk with her column of kittens swills
    the garbage pail.
She jabs her wedge-head in a cup
of sour cream, drops her ostrich tail,
and will not scare.

Lowell's accomplishment in "Skunk Hour" is to have found a tone which at once gestures toward larger meanings and yet allows for the speaker's own crippling private nightmare. The opening stanzas permit him his "fascinated disgust" with the world; the later stanzas counter any impression of self-righteousness, of easy world-weariness which the reader may be tempted to attribute to him. How much he takes to himself the skunks, the crude defiant survivors, is a difficult question. The casual half-rhymes and feminine endings do give way to more resolute and emphatic stresses at the close. The tone is partly one of amused relief and identification, though as John Berryman pointed out, it also encourages absurd contrasts between the bold skunks and the human who admits his own terror: "I will. I *do* 'scare!' " It is, at any rate, clear that in this poem Lowell moves toward a more exposed autobiographical style, one that does not mask his anger or disabilities behind apocalyptic rhetoric and social critique.

But, to see the nature of this exposure, it would help to look at a poem typical of the barer "life studies." "Memories of West Street and Lepke" shuttles back and forth between the comfortable Lowell living in Boston in the 1950s and his recall of the year he spent in a New York jail as a conscientious objector.

Only teaching on Tuesdays, book-worming
in pajamas fresh from the washer each morning,
I hog a whole house on Boston's

"hardly passionate Marlborough Street,"
where even the man
scavenging filth in the back alley trash cans,
has two children, a beach wagon, a helpmate,
and is a "young Republican."
I have a nine months' daughter,
young enough to be my granddaughter.
Like the sun she rises in her flame-flamingo infants' wear.

These are the tranquillized *Fifties*,
and I am forty. Ought I to regret my seedtime?
I was a fire-breathing Catholic C.O.,
and made my manic statement.

However plain the style, there is no mistaking the speaker for the
apparently casual observer in Elizabeth Bishop's poems. Gabriel Pearson
says of this and other *Life Studies* that "Lowell's treatment suggests not an
exhibition but a cauterization of private material and emotion. Interest is not
in what is revealed but in what is reserved." No object in the poem seems
to be allowed the independent interest often accorded by Bishop. Instead
things bristle with an accusatory significance, all too relevant to the speaker,
an "I" not at all relaxed or random in his self-presentation. So much of his
experience is already second-hand, as in his self-conscious reference to what
Henry James had long since identified as "hardly passionate Marlborough
Street," an etiolated gesture toward an etiolated frame. Experiences seem
preempted by rhetoric of the Eisenhower period ("agonizing reappraisal") or
by advertising ("Like the sun she rises in her flame-flamingo infants' wear").

He talks about himself in implied ironic quotation marks. You imagine
them around "fire-breathing" and "manic" in the lines "I was a fire-breathing
Catholic C.O., / and made my manic statement." Line endings have a similar
dry effect: "Given a year, / I walked on the roof of the West Street Jail."
The break forces a wry question; a momentary stepping back, *"given,"* in-
deed. This is the language of a man on trial, who hear words as if they
belonged to someone else. "Fire-breathing" and "manic" are overheard char-
acterizations, expressions he cannot adopt completely as his own. Prepared
reactions of the "tranquilized Fifties" encrust his responses, make it hard to
break through to feeling.

The distance between the speaker and his experience gives "Memories
of West Street and Lepke" its special tension, the air that something is being
withheld rather than yielded. So, for example, the mind seems to be making
some flickering connection between the daughter's "flame-flamingo infants'

wear" and the "seedtime" of the "fire-breathing Catholic C.O." It is a linguistic tease, not fully worked out. We are being asked to think about the "dragon" of a father, and the roseate daughter young enough to be his granddaughter, about a passage of vitality. Something is being suggested about failed ideology and the lapse into slogan-encapsulated domesticity of the 1950s and of middle age.

Gabriel Pearson tells us that in reading Lowell "we should notice how far . . . objects are re-apprehended and, as it were, redeemed for attention, by being locked and cemented into larger structures. They are never really innocent, autarchic objects like Williams's red wheelbarrow. They are there because they serve a significance or are at least apt for some design." In "Memories of West Street and Lepke," Lowell seems to take very little primary pleasure in the objects named and remembered. The "pajamas fresh from the washer each morning" seem there not so much for themselves as to prepare our curiosity for a later detail, Czar Lepke, "piling towels on a rack." It is one of several parallels, teasing us into wondering what links the speaker in his laundered world to the boss of Murder Incorporated. Lowell remembers

> the T shirted back
> of *Murder Incorporated's* Czar Lepke,
> there piling towels on a rack,
> or dawdling off to his little segregated cell full
> of things forbidden the common man:
> a portable radio, a dresser, two toy American
> flags tied together with a ribbon of Easter palm.
> Flabby, bald, lobotomized,
> he drifted in sheepish calm.

Both Lowell and Lepke belong to privileged worlds. The poet, hogging a whole house, remembers Lepke in "a segregated cell full / of things forbidden the common man." Outside, like the scavenger on Lowell's Marlborough Street, is the anarchic variety of the prison of which the younger Lowell was a part: "a Negro boy with curlicues / of marijuana in his hair"; Abramowitz, another pacifist. "Bioff and Brown, the Hollywood pimps," beat Abramowitz black and blue; it sounds like an energetic alliterative game to accompany Lowell from the tranquillized present to a busy, untidy past.

Linked to the outlaw vividness, the young man glimpsed at its forbidden center Lepke. "Flabby, bald, lobotomized, / he drifted in a sheepish calm." A *doppelgänger* for the middle-aged speaker in his tranquilized forties, Lepke is an object of fastidious envy, if only for his pure preoccupation with death. Lepke, at least, is

> where no agonizing reappraisal
> jarred his concentration on the electric chair—
> hanging like an oasis in his air
> Of lost connections.

"Agonizing reappraisals" are the thieves of experience in the poet's world; Lepke's "lost connections" open to an oasis not visible on Marlborough Street.

Or so the parallels and the patterns of the poem suggest. The arrangement of details and scenes invites us to make comparisons and contrasts upon which the poem itself deliberately makes no comment (not even to say, as Williams did, "The pure products of America go crazy"). Finally the poet's baffled failure to generalize becomes one of the subjects of the poem. The figures in the frieze have the air of being deliberately chosen and placed, deliberately recalled for the skilled analyst like key figures in a dream. Lost as the connections are between the criminal past and the respectable drugged present, the poem bristles with the challenge to recapture and unite them. Its selective organization teases us toward meaning, even if it is only in the form of a conundrum, a puzzle whose pieces we must match ourselves. Lowell pictures himself as becalmed; his poem, on the other hand, insists almost militantly on what Pearson calls the "vital chore of unremitting interrogation."

Over the years *Life Studies* has taught its readers how to interpret such poems as "Memories of West Street and Lepke," poems once characterized as random and flat. The short lines, the deliberately low-key vocabulary are ways of focusing our attention. Against such plainness a repeated gesture or word or color can take on unexpected resonance and can suggest obsessive connections between otherwise unlikely figures. "My Last Afternoon with Uncle Devereux Winslow" depends on a network of small details to reveal the fearful links between the five-and-a-half-year-old Lowell and his uncle, dying of Hodgkin's disease at twenty-nine. The child's wish to escape to imperishable death, his revulsion against his life full of relatives failing and dying—these feelings emerge slowly and by implication. It takes a reading as painstaking as Stephen Yenser's in *Circle to Circle* to interpret the seemingly meaningless details: the child picking away at a blue anchor on his white sailor blouse; the uncle also remembered in blue and white, about to "sail" for Europe on a last honeymoon before his death. The connections are latent, bristle with significance as in dreams, but as in dreams leave interpretation for afterward.

What happens within single poems happens in *Life Studies* as a whole. Poems in the opening sections throw up muted parallels and resonant images which prepare us for the Lowell autobiography in Part Four. Stephen Yenser speaks of Lowell's protagonists, some of them poets and friends, as "a line of alienated figures whose plights enforce and illuminate one another." He shows in an intricate argument the accumulating effect of figures like "A Mad Negro Soldier Confined at Munich," Ford Madox Ford and Delmore Schwartz, whose fates rhyme with one another and allow Lowell eventually to associate "madness, war, and art." How do *we* know to associate them with one another? Partly because of gathering small recurring details. (Yenser even links the "mustard spire" in "A Mad Negro Soldier" to the mustard gas in "Ford Madox Ford" and "For Delmore Schwartz.") Partly because of an almost musical construction. Yenser points out that, "In its tempo, its use of a persona whose sexual needs to testify to estrangement from society, its mood of barely restrained violence, and its acerbic tone, and even in its position at the end of a section, 'Words for Hart Crane' is related to 'A Mad Negro Soldier Confined at Munich'; and at the same time, by virtue of all these features except the tempo, it is a forerunner of 'Skunk Hour.' "

The critical reader, at some more or less conscious level, associates through memory these disparate experiences and images. It is important that the poet in his poems appears not to. Having recognized the glinting clues for what they are, he does not choose to let them come together directly in his poems. We may build readings, if only as a relief from the tension of recognizing details, situations and images which half rhyme with one another. Having done our critical detective work, having put the puzzle together, we always have to return to the poet's professed state of mind, the dispersal of clues as in a dream, the patient's report only just on the verge of interpretation. So, for example, much of the fear felt in connecting himself with Murder Incorporated's Czar Lepke must have been absorbed by the very discovery of an interrogatory structure which both linked them and kept them apart. It is Lowell's way of posing questions about his life without having, directly, to answer them.

III

Having tried to bring memories forward in *Life Studies*, Lowell often steps back to consider memory as a problem in his next book, *For the Union Dead* (1964). Writing autobiography brought with it glimpses of chaos and nightmare: Lepke's inner eye fixed on the electric chair; the crazed night cruiser of "Skunk Hour"; the infantile bravado of the mental hospital of

"Waking in the Blue." It is no wonder that Lowell so often casts himself in a distanced role, as a baffled spectator, sometimes as a voyeur. In "Skunk Hour," behind the wheel of his Tudor Ford, he watches for "love cars." In "For the Union Dead" he remembers how, as a child, he stared through the aquarium's glass walls at "the dark downward and vegetating kingdom / of the fish," his hand tingling to burst the bubbles from the "cowed, compliant fish." Later in the same poem he is pressed against a barbed-wire fence to see the "dinosaur steamshovels" devouring Boston Common for a new parking garage. At the close of that poem, crouching before his television set, he sees "the drained faces of Negro school-children rise like balloons." The postures—and the poem itself—become a screen between the poet and certain ungovernable experiences, public and private. Present and past seem equally unavailable: the "airy tanks" in the Boston Aquarium of his childhood, and the faces of black children (on the TV news?) are equally "drained." Or else, topsy-turvy, in another poem the poet himself drifts powerless and protected: "I swim like a minnow / behind my studio window." This is one image he finds for his baffled reaction to the talk, "the chafe and jar / of nuclear war" in "Fall 1961."

It is clear even from a few examples that *For the Union Dead* includes a network of observers and observed, one or the other behind glass. "The state / is a diver under a glass bell" ("Fall 1961"). The poems stand by themselves, but they also accumulate, in waves of concentration and dispersal, a series of associations with eyesight and vision. At the center of the book are accounts of nightmares and dreams which have to do with the eyeglasses put aside at night, with eye injuries and the memories they recall. In "Myopia: A Night," without his glasses' aid and screen, Lowell moves into a dream world of the present tense: "ramshackle, streaky, weird / for the near-sighted." Its white "cell of learning" gives no relief.

> I hoped
> its blank, foregoing whiteness
> would burn away the blur,
> as my five senses clenched
> their teeth, thought stitched to thought,
> as through a needle's eye.

Instead he finds a dazzling Lucifer in his room, while his family's faces blur. "What has disturbed this household?"

In "The Flaw" he suffers from a mote in the eye (a hair on a contact lens?) and in "Eye and Tooth" an eye injury recalls an "old cut cornea."

These too are ways of exploring and exposing his fragile position. In "Eye
and Tooth":

> My whole eye was sunset red,
> the old cut cornea throbbed,
> I saw things darkly,
> as through an unwashed goldfish globe.

The lens through which he sees is a terrifying and necessary one. Seeing
things "darkly," a parody prophet, he is both protected from and given
carefully limited access to memories of an earlier lens:

> No ease for the boy at the keyhole,
> his telescope,
> when the women's white bodies flashed
> in the bathroom. Young, my eyes began to fail.

A physical affliction, by laconic juxtaposition, turns into a comment on
childhood sexuality. The punishment is biblical, too, an echo of what Moses
prophesies for the dispersed children of Israel. Matching the inflamed eye
of the poet is the eye of a "sharp-shinned hawk" remembered from a birdbook,
another strict reminder of the biblical laws of the fathers:

> clasping the abstract imperial sky.
> It says:
> *an eye for an eye,*
> *a tooth for a tooth.*

Memories of childhood are seldom innocent for Lowell. They almost
always twin complicity (here, a boy's erotic games) and powerlessness (here,
before the fantasy punishment). "No ease," the poem keeps saying. The
adult present is described in past tenses. It is a shift to the present tense that
brings back boyhood memories and threatens to overwhelm. "Eye and
Tooth," like "Myopia," is a haunted poem, an extreme version of the baffled
eye through which Lowell sees most experience in this volume. At some
points flawed vision seems a punishment for opening ungovernable ranges
of feeling. It can also be his protection. "In "Eye and Tooth," "I saw things
darkly, / as through an unwashed goldfish globe." What keeps "Eye and
Tooth" together is that frail self-assertion, a tainted prophet who sets himself
against the almost invincible Mosaic prophecies of his family which fill the
rest of the poem. At the outset he is jaunty and self-deprecating, a neglected
minnow in his unwashed bowl, or perhaps the ghost of a touring gypsy with
a makeshift crystal ball. At the close he is wearied and wearying.

"Eye and Tooth" is a gloss on a pitiful and precarious situation. The book of which it is a part lifts often toward an optative mood, a wish to be transported back to immune pleasures of childhood. At least three times in *For the Union Dead* he invites someone or himself, directly, to "Remember." At other points, as in "The Lesson," the wish surfaces as exclamation and regret:

> No longer to lie reading *Tess of the d'Urbervilles*,
> while the high, mysterious squirrels
> rain small green branches on our sleep!

But the hedged wish is as far as he will go. He recalls "Those Before Us" warily, "in the corners of the eye," not straight on. Talking about those figures who lived in a familiar house is almost involuntary. They are "uniformly gray . . . They never were." Is this a way of keeping them securely dead? Or, as Stephen Yenser suggests, a sign of their vitality when they were alive: they never merely *were*. In either case they represent spectral figures to whom only momentary homage is offered. ("Bless the confidence / of their sitting unguarded there in stocking feet.") Where he must be "guarded," they are not. However much he wants to deny them, they are present: "But in the silence, / some one lets out his belt to breathe, some one / roams in negligee." There is a moment of danger and violence in this uncontrollable past: "The muskrat that took a slice of your thumb still huddles." It "furiously slashed to matchwood" a packing crate, and, as a kind of surrogate for the child, "learned to wait / for us playing dead" in a tin wastebasket, before lashing out in terror. Powerlessness and complicity. In grudging tribute to the family ghosts, "We follow their gunshy shadows down the trail," part of their dying life. The end takes place in that limbo where Lowell would like to cast most of his memories: "Pardon them for existing. / We have stopped watching them. They have stopped watching." The mixture of regret and relief is inescapable; the senses of "watch" multiply from *wariness* to *care*.

IV

Lowell recalls—with as much gusto as T. S. Eliot marshalled to say it—a remark the older New England poet made to him at Harvard.

> "Don't you loathe to be compared with your relatives?
> I do. I've just found two of mine reviewed by Poe.
> He wiped the floor with them . . . and I was *delighted*."

Mischief is one way of handling the problem; insistence on an embalmed past is more often Lowell's. Memory, however much he craves it, never has a nourishing or regenerative force for Lowell, never the reviving power it has, classically, for Proust. There are no madeleines in this world, only a past which has already been consumed. It is for this reason that many of the poems turn toward elegy. "Always inside me is the child who died, / always inside me is his will to die."

The lines are from "Night Sweat" and are followed by the powerful, mysterious, idiosyncratic metaphor that Lowell develops for the passage of memory into art: "one universe, one body . . . in this urn / the animal night sweats of the spirit burn." A resonant couplet, the emphatic close of the first two sonnets that make up this poem, the lines force together grim contradictory feelings. The "urn" contains the spent ashes of a dead childhood and, at the same time, the fevers of creation and nightmare. As the shell of the body, it is devoured by what it burns; as the urn of memory or verse, it preserves what is destroyed. If the lines are about transformation, the stress falls on what is consumed. What he captures is a fascinated repugnance. These are "the animal night sweats of the *spirit*," as if the Latin meanings ("spirit," "breath") behind the English *animal* were just barely still alive.

The images of "Night Sweat" are explored, and perhaps even generated, in the childhood recollections of "The Neo-Classical Urn," a poem printed earlier in the volume. It recalls, as Poirier says, "youthful callousness in which the poet recognizes his kinship both with 'turtles' and with the 'urn' in which, as a child, he threw them to suffer and die. The discovery of this metaphorical connection is itself the subject of the poem, as startling to the poet as it is to us." The poetic stakes are high. He addresses the garden urn as if it were something out of Keats: "Oh neo-classical white urn, Oh nymph, / Oh lute!" The childhood he remembers at first sounds like an echo of Wordsworth, breathless, exhilarated, in a "season of joy":

> Rest!
> I could not rest. At full run on the curve,
> I left the cast stone statue of a nymph,
> her soaring armpits and her one bare breast,
> gray from the rain and graying in the shade,
> as on, on, in sun, the pathway now a dyke,
> I swerved between two water bogs,
> two seins of moss, and stopped to snatch
> the paint turtles on dead logs.

If this is Wordsworthian elation, it is rebuked as the turtles the boy collects are "dropped splashing in our garden urn." The Wordsworthian catch falls into a Keatsian vessel "like money in the bank." The deflated allusions are there to suggest that romantic notions about childhood nourishing poetry are inadequate for this particular poet. His classical urn leads him to a new and terrifying version of the consumption of experience by art.

The poem moves along toward its remorseless discoveries with a series of separated but timely rhymes: childhood experience *hummed*; the pitiless boy who *strummed* the drowned beasts' elegy; the turtles which "popped up dead on the stale *scummed* / surface." The skull which recalls and which disowns its dead animal spirits is finally faced with acknowledging them as its own:

> nothings! Turtles! I rub my skull,
> that turtle shell,
> and breathe their dying smell,
> still watch their crippled last survivors pass,
> and hobble humpbacked through the grizzled grass.

A kinship is owned by the ambiguous subject of the last line (*turtles*, the first meaning, but also, the poet). Linked to "Night Sweat," the misery becomes clearer: "Always inside me is the child who died." The strenuous self-reflections in these poems are Lowell's deepest reports on an imagined monstrousness transformed, but not concealed or atoned, by art. This is, after all, the book in which he writes about his childhood identification with Caligula, the source of his nickname Cal.

So exposed, the sense of complicity and guilt rubs off on all relationships. In "Night Sweat" the tenderness with which he addresses his wife is touched by something else as well:

> your lightness alters everything,
> and tears the black web from the spider's sack,
> as your heart hops and flutters like a hare.
> Poor turtle, tortoise, if I cannot clear
> the surface of these troubled waters here,
> absolve me, help me, Dear Heart, as you bear
> this world's dead weight and cycle on your back.

Contact with his wife and child, with approaching day, is colored by shame and a plea for absolution. That much is clear, as is the reference back to the drowned turtles of "The Neo-Classical Urn." It remains a mystery whether "Poor turtle, tortoise" is a self-description (*tortoise*: the weighty antipode of the "hare" in the preceding line), in apposition to the drowning "I," or whether it is an endearment to his wife, an appeal touched by guilt. (In that case, the turtle which bears the universe on its back.) In either case, an openness to the self-consuming, even murderous animal spirits of the past has exhausted him.

These "night sweats" are partly the product of seeing ghosts. Memory of and by itself does not animate the present for him, as it does for writers like Wordsworth and Proust. On the contrary, it threatens to overwhelm him, to cut him off from the present and from his living wife and daughter. What are for other writers revitalizing links to childhood are not for Lowell one of the keys to an acknowledged and shared humanity. To redeem himself from monstrousness and isolation is to recognize the decaying mind and body as his links to humankind. The skull in "The Neo-Classical Urn" is the cerebral skull which at once consumes the animal spirits and is itself a death's head. In the tenderer, more human version of "Night Sweat" the urn of writing is also the body, self-consuming, self-embalming.

What I am getting at is that autobiography for Lowell is a problematic form. He probes the reasons unflinchingly in these exposed dream poems at the center of *For the Union Dead*. Involuntary memory won't do. It is more congenial for him to write autobiography from the point of view of the elegist—experiencing himself and others almost entirely as members of Yeats's "dying generations." "In truth," he says, "I seem to have felt mostly the joys of living; in remembering, in recording, thanks to the gift of the Muse, it is the pain." Lowell gets a tainted joy from the notion that he is "reborn" in his writing. That discovery is repeated again and again in his work, most beautifully much later in *Notebook* and *History* in "Reading Myself":

> No honeycomb is built without a bee
> adding circle to circle, cell to cell,
> the wax and honey of a mausoleum—
> this round dome proves its maker is alive;
> the corpse of the insect lives embalmed in honey,
> prays that its perishable work live long
> enough for the sweet-tooth bear to desecrate—
> this open book . . . my open coffin.

HELEN VENDLER

Last Days and Last Poems

The last years of Robert Lowell's life, when I knew him, were ones of almost emblematic location. He and his wife, Caroline Blackwood, were in Kent in a manor house called Milgate Park; when that house was sold, they lived at Castletown House in Ireland; he taught at Harvard one term each year, giving a course in nineteenth- or twentieth-century poetry and holding open office hours in which he commented on the writing of those presenting work; he was, during his last summer, in Maine with his second wife, Elizabeth Hardwick. In England and Ireland he was an expatriate; at Harvard he was at home by virtue of birth and name but exotic by virtue of his life and his poetry; in Maine he was returning to a scene long-familiar. In his final summer he went for the first time to Russia. After his sudden death on his return from Ireland to New York, there was a funeral at his childhood church, the Church of the Advent, not far from the Revere Street which appears in *Life Studies*. Finally, he was buried in the Winslow and Stark family cemetery, still in Dunbarton, New Hampshire, though moved from the original location described in several of his poems.

These various places—Boston, Maine, England, Ireland, New York—the old-fashioned, the urban, the rural, the foreign, the sophisticated—respond to facets of Lowell's complex character and appear in his last poems, collected in *Day by Day* (1977). In these poems Lowell becomes not only the New England poet of Boston, Dunbarton, and Maine, not only the American poet of New York, Washington, and Ohio, but also the expatriate poet of

From *Part of Nature, Part of Us: Modern American Poetry.* © 1980 by the President and Fellows of Harvard College. Harvard University Press, 1980.

Kent and Ireland. Besides new places he added new experiences, writing for
the first time at any length as the father of a son—a son uncannily resembling
him. He wrote of physical illness—he was hospitalized briefly in January
1977 for congestive heart disease—an of the expectation, not unfounded, of
his death.

Like the books which preceded it, *Day by Day* was attacked. "Slack and
meretricious," one fellow poet said of the later poetry, accusing it of "the
lassitude and despondency of self-imitation." In twenty years, he prophesied,
no one would praise *Day by Day*, which would remain "a sad footnote to the
corruption of a great poet." Without attempting to usurp the function of
time, which will decide whether *Day by Day* is a stern and touching volume,
as I believe it to be, or whether it deserves no such praise, I would like to
dwell on a few of its poems and a few of its claims, beginning with its own
description of itself. But I must look first, briefly, at its predecessors.

Lowell began as a writer of an obscure and oblique poetry, which
struggled violently with murky feeling, invented baffling displaced sufferings
like those in *The Mills of the Kavanaughs*, resisted interpretation, and discovered
original resources in traditional forms. This poetry, in spite of its difficulty,
attracted wide attention and praise, so much so that its very strength was
the greatest obstacle to Lowell's poetic progress. *Life Studies* disappointed
readers attached to Lowell's earlier "Catholic" manner, and the lean and
loose-jointed poems which are now his most famous work had to wait some
time for popular acceptance. Just as *Life Studies* entered the anthologies,
Lowell returned to a species of formality, writing innumerable sonnets (col-
lected in *Notebook* and subsequent volumes), compressing life with what
seemed extraordinary cruelty and candor into a Procrustean and unyielding
shape. These poems have not yet been assimilated—except in a voyeuristic
way—into the American literary consciousness. "It takes ten years," Lowell
said dryly of popular acquiescence.

Now he has ended, in *Day by Day*, as a writer of disarming openness,
exposing shame and uncertainty, offering almost no purchase to interpre-
tation, and in his journal-keeping, abandoning conventional structure,
whether rhetorical or logical. The poems drift from one focus to another;
they avoid the histrionic; they sigh more often than they expostulate. They
acknowledge exhaustion; they expect death. Admirers of the sacerdotal and
autocratic earlier manner are offended by this diminished diarist, this sud-
denly quiescent volcano. But Lowell knew better than anyone else what he
had given up: "Those blessed structures, plot and rhyme— / why are they
no help to me now," he begins his closing poem, "Epilogue." He had been
willing to abandon plot and rhyme in writing about things recalled—in order

to make that recall casual and natural. But now, in his last poem, he wanted "to make something imagined, not recalled," and wished to return to plot and rhyme. But the habit of the volume held, and the last testament is unrhymed and unplotted, as unstructured apparently as its companions. Despairingly, Lowell contrasts himself with the "true" artists, the painter, feeling himself to be like Hawthorne's Coverdale, only an American dageurrotypist:

> Sometimes everything I write
> with the threadbare art of my eye
> seems a snapshot,
> lurid, rapid, garish, grouped,
> heightened from life,
> yet paralyzed by fact.

Lowell here anticipates all that could be said, and has been said, in criticism of his last book: that his art does not go clothed in the gorgeous tapestry of his earlier work, but is threadbare; that he is making capital of the lurid and garish episodes of his life—adolescent cruelty, family scandal, madness, three marriages; that his poems are rapid sketches rather than finished portraits; that he is hampered by his allegiance to fact without even the compensating virtue of absolute truthfulness, since all is heightened by compression and focus. After this devastating self-criticism, the only self-defense can be the anti-bourgeois question "Yet why not say what happened?"

Howard Nemerov has called the poet "the weak criminal whose confession implicates the others": and Lowell's "saying what happened" is not a cowardice of the imagination but a subversive heroism of the memory. "Memory is genius," Lowell said once at a reading, regretting how little remained even in his own prodigious memory, and regretting as well the poverty of language as a vehicle for the preservation of the past:

> How quickly I run through my little set
> of favored pictures . . . pictures starved to words.
> My memory economizes so prodigally
> I know I have suffered theft.

Abandoning the showy "objective correlatives" for his life which fill the earlier poetry. Lowell prays in his last poem for the "grace of accuracy," which he found in the Dutch realists, from Van Eyck to Vermeer. There is in this volume a painstaking description of Van Eyck's Arnolfini marriage portrait. The couple are not beautiful: the husband stands "long-faced and dwindling," the wife is pregnant; the husband "lifts a hand, / thin and white as his face / held up like a candle to bless her . . . / they are rivals in homeliness and love." In the background of the portrait, Lowell sees all the furniture of their common life: "The picture is too much like their life— / a crisscross, too many petty facts"; a candelabrum, peaches, the husband's wooden shoes "thrown on the floor by her smaller ones," the bed, "the restless marital canopy." This "petty" domestic inclusiveness is what Lowell now proposes to write about in place of his former metaphysical blazes, even in place of his former carefully casual "life studies." We know at least, then, that the aesthetic of the last work was not an unconscious or an unconsidered one. Whether it is, as some would say, a rationalization after the fact, justifying, *faute de mieux*, an exhausted invention, only history can tell; some will see in these pieces a shrewdness of choice and an epigrammatic wit that suggest consummate art.

These last poems, so random-seeming, were nonetheless composed with Lowell's characteristic severity of self-criticism. The worksheets, as always, are innumerable, incessant. Lowell lived for writing, was never happier than, as he said, when revising his revisions. Successive versions were exposed to the criticism of friends; spurred by questions, objections, suggestions, he would return eagerly to his drafts, and change, transpose, rewrite. "He loved to tinker," he said of God; it was equally true of himself. His brilliant adjectives were not achieved by chance; his inspired aphorisms took time to perfect themselves. His manuscripts may be the most interesting since Yeats's.

Lowell died in September 1977, at sixty. To honor his birthday, and commemorate his death, the Houghton Library of Harvard University exhibited a selection from his papers on deposit there. His unremitting work appears in his earliest notebooks, in the drafts for such famous poems as "The Quaker Graveyard" (originally entitled "To Herman Melville") and "Skunk Hour" (which had begun as a poem of personal desolation but had acquired, late, its first three stanzas of tolerant, if biting, social description). The Houghton exhibit included a letter Lowell wrote, at eighteen, to his father, declaring his vocation as a writer: "If I fail at this, I would fail at anything else," he wrote, as I recall the page.

How, then, are we to read these late poems? Not, certainly, for the blessed structures of plot and rhyme; not for the hard-driving compression of the late sonnets; not for the transforming and idealizing power of lyric; not for the diamond certainties of metaphysical verse; not for the retrospective and elegiac stationing of figures as in *Life Studies*; not for the visionary furies of youth. One afternoon in spring, I walked with Lowell through Harvard Yard. "Did you see that Christopher Ricks had written a piece about me?"

he said. "No, what did he say?" I asked. "He said I'm violent," said Lowell
with a mixture of humor and irony. "And Ehrenpreis says you're comic," I
said. "Why don't they ever say what I'd like them to say?" he protested.
"What's that?" I asked. "That I'm heartbreaking," he said, meaning it.

And so he is. If this book is read, as it should be, as a journal, written
"day by day," as a fragment of an autobiography (Lowell called his poems
"my verse autobiography"), it is heartbreaking. It records his late, perhaps
unwise, third marriage; the birth of a son; the very worst memories sup-
pressed from *Life Studies*, memories of having been an unwanted child and
a tormented adolescent; exile in Britain and Ireland; the death of friends;
clinical depression and hospitalization, lovemaking and impotence; distress
over age; fear of death. Against all this is set the power of writing—"universal
consolatory / description without significance, / transcribed verbatim by my
eye."

Readers who demand something more than the eye's verbatim tran-
script, who do not ask whether in fact there is anything more, may not find
these poems heartbreaking. But the Wordsworth who said that the meanest
flower that blows could give thoughts that do often lie too deep for tears
would, I think, understand the tears underlying these "petty facts" of one
man's existence. Let me quote some of Lowell's memorable descriptions.

Of sexual impotence, recalling sexual capacity: "Last summer nothing
dared impede / the flow of the body's thousand rivulets of welcome." "Riv-
ulets" is, in its pastoral and Wordsworthian tenderness, the word carrying
all the delicacy of reference. On depression: "a wooden winter shadow,"
with the paralysis of that state hiding in the word "wooden." On ants, and
their pragmatic and logical errands: "They are lost case of the mind." On
death: "My eyes flicker, the immortal / is scraped unconsenting from the
mortal." On old age: "We learn the spirit is very willing to give up, / but
the body is weak and will not die." On the anticipation of his own death
and burial:

> In a church,
> the Psalmist's glass mosaic Shepherd
> and bright green pastures
> seem to wait
> with the modish faithlessness
> and erotic daydream
> of art nouveau for our funeral.

And yet, for all their air of verbatim description, these poems, like all
poems, are invented things. They are invented even in little. Lowell once
handed me a draft of a new poem, called "Bright Day in Boston." It begins,

"Joy of standing up my dentist, / X-ray plates like a broken Acropolis . . . / Joy to idle through Boston." I was struck by the *panache* of standing up one's dentist, and said so; "Well, as a matter of fact," said Lowell sheepishly, "I actually *did* go to the dentist first, and *then* went for the walk." But in the poem, "the unpolluted joy / And criminal leisure of a boy"—to quote earlier verses—became fact, where in life they had been only wish. The life of desire is as evident in these poems as the life of fact. Medical prescriptions are both named and rejected: "What is won by surviving, / if two glasses of red wine are poison?" The Paterian interval becomes ever smaller: "We only live between / before we are and what we were." Lowell looks in terror to "the hungry future, / the time when any illness is chronic, / and the years of discretion are spent on complaint— / . . . until the wristwatch is taken from the wrist." These deathly truths, unrelieved by any prospect of afterlife or immortality, are, I think, what dismay many readers. How squalid and trivialized a view of death, they may feel—chronic illness, complaint, and that last hospital gesture, the wristwatch taken from the wrist. But over against that end, Lowell sets a flickering terrestrial Eden: "We took our paradise here—how else love?" That "a man love[s] a woman more than women" remained for him an insoluble and imprisoning mystery: "A man without a wife / is like a turtle without a shell." "Nature," says Lowell who is part of nature, "is sundrunk with sex," but he would "seek leave unimpassioned by [his] body." That leave was not granted him: he stayed with women till the end of the party, "a half-filled glass in each hand— / . . . swayed / by the hard infatuate wine of love."

In this last accuracy the poet cannot even see himself as unique, unusual, set apart. There is the humility of the generic about this volume, in spite of its pride in its poetic work. As far as he can see, Lowell tells us, each generation leads the same life, the life of its time. No one in the present is wiser or more foolish than those in the past or the future. No fresh perfection treads on our heels; nor do we represent any decay of nature. This attitude distresses those who come to poetry for hope, transcendence, the inspiriting word. "Really," says Lowell to Berryman in his elegy for Berryman, "we had the same life / the generic one / our generation offered." First they were students, then they, as teachers themselves, had students; they had their *grands maîtres* as all young writers do, they had their "fifties' fellowships / to Paris, Rome and Florence," they were "veterans of the Cold War not the War." Thousands of other intellectuals of their generation had the same "generic life." If he were young now, says Lowell, he would be indistinguishable from the other young, listening to rock, "lost / in unreality and loud music."

In a class lecture on Arnold, Lowell once said that "Dover Beach" had been criticized, "in the old days of the New Critics," for not continuing the sea imagery in the last stanza; "But I think by then," Lowell went on, "you've had quite enough of it." His sense of the fluidity of life's events and of human response pressed him into some of the same discontinuity of imagery, and drew the disapproval of purists in structure. Lowell believed—I am quoting another class—that the poem "is an event, not the record of an event"; "the lyric claims to produce an event; it is this for which it strives and which it sometimes brings off." Like an event, the lyric can be abrupt, odd-shaped, irregularly featured, and inconclusive. The important thing is the presence of "exciting or strenuous writing"—what one finds in Henry James, he said, on every page, good or bad. Power and wistfulness stood, for Lowell, in inverse relation: he praised the "tender" poems at the end of *Leaves of Grass* while remarking nonetheless how different in tone Whitman's later poetry, written when he was ill, was from the poetry of his "great healthy days." We might say the same of Lowell's last collection. The impetuousness of the "manic statement" is gone: mania is now viewed with apprehension and horror: "I grow too merry, / when I stand in my nakedness to dress." Even poetry itself can seem to want conviction: it becomes merely a compulsive "processing of words," a "dull instinctive glow," refueling itself from "bits of paper brought to feed it," which it blackens.

In the transparent myth which opens *Day by Day*, a weary Ulysses tires of Circe, returns to a deformed Ithaca, to a Penelope corrupted by living well, and finds rage his only authentic and vivid emotion. A shorthand of reference is substituted for the luxuries of description, while a desultory motion replaces youth's arrowy energy. No one would deny that this poetry has destructive designs on convention. Lowell once quoted Eliot on Coleridge: "By the time he wrote the *Biographia Literaria* he was a ruin, but being a ruin is a sort of occupation." (T. S. Eliot actually wrote in *The Use of Poetry and the Use of Criticism*: "Sometimes, however, to be 'a ruined man' is itself a vocation.") The remark reveals a good deal about Eliot, but Lowell's citation is interesting in itself: it conveys the conviction of the artist-survivor that there is always something to be made of life, even of its orts and offal, its tired ends, its disappointments and disgusts, its ironies. The sense of the end of life must find some expression, even if in what Stevens called "long and sluggish lines." Without endorsing an imitative form, we can yet find in Lowell's casualness, his waywardness, his gnomic summaries, his fragmentary reflections, authentic representations of a sixty-year-old memory.

Not every poem, I suppose, succeeds in giving "each figure in the photograph / his living name." But the poet who had decided that "we are

poor passing facts" felt obliged to a poetry of deprivation and of transient
actuality, lit up by moments of unearthly pained happiness, like that in his
last aubade:

> For the last two minutes, the returning monarchy
> of the full moon looks down on the first chirping sparrows—
> nothing lovelier than waking to find
> another breathing body in my bed . . .
> glowshadow halfcovered with dayclothes like my own,
> caught in my arms.

The poetry of "poor passing facts" entails the sacrifice in large part of two
aspects of Lowell's poetry that had brought him many admirers: his large
reference to European literature, through his allusions and translations
(which he called "Imitations"); and his political protest. In that earlier gran-
deur of literary scope, as well as by the moral grandeur of defiance and
protest, Lowell seemed to claim a vision and power for poetry that many
readers were happy to see affirmed. Others were more pleased by the de-
velopment, beginning in *For the Union Dead* and culminating in Lowell's final
volume, of a humbler style, that of a man, in Rolando Anzilotti's fine de-
scription, "who confronts directly and with courage his own failures, his
faults and despairings, without seeking comfort, without indicating solutions
to cling to. Feeling is revealed with the subtlest delicacy and candor, in its
essential being." "The eye of Lowell for the particular which becomes uni-
versal," Anzilotti continues, "is precise and perfect; . . . we are far away
from the oratory, from the bursting out of emotion in tumultuous rhythms,
that appeared in 'The Quaker Graveyard.' " This line of writing, as Anzilotti
points out, remained in equilibrium with the national and moral concerns
evident in *Near the Ocean* and *Notebook*; not until this final volume did the
precise eye and the quotidian feeling become the dominant forces in Lowell's
aesthetic. The allusions in this last collection come from an occasional back-
ward glance to favorite passages—a line of Dante, a line of Horace—but the
poetic mind turns less and less to past literature, more and more to the
immediacy of present event. There is only one poem in the volume that
springs from a political impetus; "Fetus," prompted by the trial, in Boston,
of a doctor accused of making no effort to keep an aborted fetus alive. And
even the poem quickly leaves its occasion behind and engages in a general
meditation on death, that "black arrow" arriving like a calling-card "on the
silver tray." It is perhaps significant that this poem is the least successful,
to my mind, in the group, in part because Lowell no longer has to hand the
moral sureness to condemn or approve the abortion. He sees only the gro-

tesquerie of the medical procedure, of the trial court, and of the biological shape of "the fetus, the homunculus, / already at four months one pound, / with shifty thumb in mouth— / . . . Our little model . . . " A poem which, by its title, "George III," might seem to be prompted by Anglo-American relations turns out, in the event, to be in part a reflection on Nixon but even more a reflection on a fate Lowell feared for himself: a permanent lapse into madness, like George,

> who whimsically picked the pockets of his page
> he'd paid to sleep all day outside his door;
> who dressed like a Quaker, who danced a minuet
> with his appalled apothecary in Kew Gardens;

who dismayed "his retinue by formally bowing to an elm, / as if it were the Chinese emissary." George's later mania bears a strong resemblance to phases of Lowell's own illness:

> addressing imaginary congresses,
> reviewing imaginary combat troops,
>
> . . . .
>
> Old, mad, deaf, half-blind,
> he talked for thirty-two hours
> on everything, everybody,
>
> read Cervantes and the Bible aloud
> simultaneously with shattering rapidity.

Social forms disappear in this last phase of Lowell's writing, and public moral witness disappears with them. The solitary human being, his life extending only as far as the domestic circle, becomes the topic of attention. Epic ambition is resigned: the *Odyssey* is reduced to a marital triangle. The personal is seen as the locus of truth, insight, and real action.

And when Lowell writes about the personal, he spares himself nothing, not the patronizing doctor in the asylum addressing Caroline, "A model guest . . . we would welcome / Robert back to Northampton any time"; not the susurrus of public or private comment about madness having attacked him even in this third, scandalous marriage:

> *If he has gone mad with her,*
> *the poor man can't have been very happy,*
> *seeing too much and feeling it*
> *with one skin-layer missing;*

nor a murderously detached self-portrait among the other mad:

> I am a thorazined fixture
> in the immovable square-cushioned chairs
> we preoccupy for seconds like migrant birds.

After the scene-setting in the asylum comes the distracted interior mono-
logue, much as it had in "Skunk Hour." But whereas in the earlier poem
the poses struck were tragic, and then comic, redeemed in some way by the
animal appetite of the skunks, the monologue in the asylum, forebodingly
called "Home," is one of pure childlike pathos:

> The immovable chairs have swallowed up the patients,
> and speak with the eloquence of emptiness.
> By each the same morning paper lies unread:
> *January 10, 1976.*
> I cannot sit or stand two minutes,
> yet walk imagining a dialogue
> between the devil and myself,
> not knowing which is which or worse,
> saying,
> as one would instinctively say Hail Mary,
> *I wish I could die.*
> Less than ever I expect to be alive
> six months from now—
> *1976,*
> a date I dare not affix to my grave.
> The Queen of Heaven, I miss her,
> we were divorced. She never doubted
> the divided, stricken soul
> could call her Maria,
> and rob the devil with a word.

The grand drama of the manic has ended, and it is the depressive side
of illness, without the illusions of mania, which gives its tone to these latter
poems. As the horizon narrows, the smallest sensations of living—waking
up alive, seeing the spring—suffice. "I thank God," says Lowell, "for being
alive— / a way of writing I once thought heartless." Heartless because selfish,
solipsistic—or so he thought when he was young, and had heart for all the
world, or so it seemed. Recognizing the fury of political statement as a
displacement of fury against parents, he can no longer permit its unmediated
and thoughtless energy. In the poem to his mother, he admits, "It has taken

me the time since you died / to discover you are as human as I am . . . / if
I am." In the poem to his father, he confesses,

> It would take two lifetimes
> to pick the crust
> and uncover the face
> under our two menacing,
> iconoclastic masks.

His father refuses the sympathy proffered when Lowell implies that now
he understands his father's life through the similarity of his own life to that
of his father: "It can't be that, / it's your life," says his father, "and dated
like mine." The failure of Lowell's father is reflected in his own failure, just
as Lowell's childhood innocence is reflected in the innocence of his little son:

> We could see clearly
> and all the same things
> before the glass was hurt.

> Past fifty, we learn with surprise and a sense
> of suicidal absolution
> that what we intended and failed
> could never have happened—
> and must be done better.

The old paternal hope that the child's life will be lived better struggles with
the conviction that each generation repeats the generic life of all its prede-
cessors. The very motive for action is removed by such resignation to the
common fate.

Nothing remains for Lowell, then, after he has jettisoned formal reli-
gious belief, social protest, a twenty-year marriage, even residence in Amer-
ica, except memory and the present moment. When asked why he wanted
a formal funeral in the Episcopal church, Lowell said, "That's how we're
buried"—that was the custom of the family. At the funeral his second and
third wives, his grown daughter and his small son, and his three stepdaugh-
ters, sat in the first mourners' pew, existing side by side as they did in his
life and his poetry. He is buried in Dunbarton next to his father and his
mother. His parents' tombstones bear inscriptions he composed; in an odd
flash of authorship, he had a signature incised, in cursive script, below the
Roman lettering—"R. Lowell Jr." There were memorial services for him in
New York, at Harvard, and in London. When Vozneszhensky came to
America, he asked to be driven to Lowell's grave, and laid on it berries

which had grown above the grave of Pasternak. Already there have been elegies, though none perhaps equal to the many elegies he wrote for the friends who preceded him in death.

In writing this last volume, Lowell pleased himself, listening with some inner ear to the inner life of the poem, deciding with mysterious certainty when it was finished, when it had found its equilibrium. I think that the instinctive principles on which he worked will become clearer with time. One writes poetry, he said, by instinct and by ear, and his own instincts and ear were pressing toward a poetry ever more unconventional, ever less "literary." He admired the way Coleridge, in his ballads, could be "showily simple and get away with it." He sought that ostentatious simplicity himself. He added that though Coleridge's verse epistle to Sara Hutchinson—the first version of the Dejection Ode—was embarrassing, yet it was "a long apologetic masterpiece—something is lost by making it an ode." What is lost is the spontaneity, the heartbreak, the domestic anguish—and that all appears in Lowell's journal written day by day. No doubt it could all have been transformed into odes; that was his old manner. But the something that was lost in such a case now seemed to him more precious than the something that is found. His last book, however casual it may seem, it not a collection of unconsidered trifles. Lowell wrote justly: "My eyes have seen what my hand did." His metaphor for this book was not one of arrangement, but one of accumulation:

> This is riches:
> the eminence not to be envied,
> the account
> accumulating layer and angle,
> face and profile,
> 50 years of snapshots,
> the ladder of ripening likeness.

If, to Lowell in a Shakespearean mood, we are "poor passing facts," in a more Keatsian moment we resemble the "camelion-poet":

> We are things thrown in the air
> alive in flight . . .
> our rust the color of the chameleon.

"Not to console or sanctify," says Stevens, speaking of the aim of modern poetry, "but plainly to propound." The plain propounding—of things thrown in the air, alive in flight, and rusting in change to the color of dust— if too severe, for some tastes, is to others profoundly assuaging. We are lucky in America in our poetry of old age: Whitman's, Stevens's, and now Lowell's. Such poetry never can speak to the young and form their sensibilities as can the poetry of passion and hope and revolutionary ardor; but it sums up another phase of life, no less valuable, no less moving, no less true.

STEVEN GOULD AXELROD

Starting Over: Learning from Williams

We study to utter our painful secret.
—EMERSON, "The Poet"

—Were you up here last night?
Yes.
What were you doing?
Writing.
What did you write?
The story of my life—
—*The Autobiography*
of William Carlos Williams

For Lowell the 1950s were a time of parental death, marital strain, and recurrent mental illness. Beginning in 1949 he had become subject to episodes of severe manic-depression, which in 1954 began to occur "once yearly," causing him to check in at regular intervals to McLean's hospital outside Boston. Rooted in the emotional conflicts of his early childhood, Lowell's illness included periods of manic delusions and erratic behavior, but its most characteristic symptom was a hollow despondency in which "one wakes, is happy for about two minutes, probably less, and then fades into dread of the day." Depression being "no gift from the muse," he found himself unable to write.

Indeed, Lowell's growing sense of artistic failure may well have contributed to his intense depression. The creative crisis which had been implicit in *The Mills of the Kavanaughs* was now upon him. In reviewing that volume, his friend Jarrell had satirically pictured him "gritting his teeth and working

From *Robert Lowell: Life and Art.* © 1978 by Princeton University Press.

away at All the Things He Does Best." Lowell felt the justice of this remark and, fearing repetition and mannerism, reduced himself to silence: "I didn't want to go just cranking the same machine." He later described the years following *The Mills of the Kavanaughs* as "six or seven years ineptitude—a slack of eternity. I remember a cousin proving to someone that I was finished—at only thirty-nine! Five Messy poems in five years!" The "five messy poems" were actually seven: early versions of the poems that eventually appeared as parts one and three of *Life Studies*. In their original versions, these poems seemed to Lowell symbol-ridden and obscure. After their appearance in little magazines in 1953 and 1954, he published no poetry at all. Curiously enough, his problem during this period was essentially technical. Lacking a language and prosody with which to express his inspiration, he lacked inspiration itself. He wrote letters to Allen Tate filled with complaints against "this old jungle of used equipment" and "the inertia of our old rhetorics and habits." But Tate could no longer help him. Lowell obliquely described his dilemma in an interview years later: "It's a terrible struggle, because what you really feel hasn't got the form, it's not what you can put down in a poem. And the poem you're equipped to write concerns nothing that you care very much about." In truth, he was in painful transit from the use of tight metrical forms, which could no longer contain and express his experience, to free verse, which could.

Even in the late 1940s, Lowell had been developing an esthetic of plain speech quite contrary to his own practice at that time. In an essay written in 1948, he said: "How few modern poems—however obscure, fierce, sonorous, pretentious, million-dollar worded—have the distinction of good conversation. . . . Literary people as a rule have less of their own to say and consequently use words with less subtlety and precision than a Maine farmer." During this same period, he praised Elizabeth Bishop and William Carlos Williams for the plainness of their language and condemned Dylan Thomas (whose style rather resembled Lowell's own) for his excessive "rhetoric." Lowell was clearly at odds with his own style of poetry for at least a decade before *Life Studies*. It is no accident that when, in the summer of 1957, he finally turned to free verse, he entitled his first effort "Inspiration." In this unpublished version of "Skunk Hour," the poet pictures himself "writing verses like a Turk," inspired by the ugly, brute reality around and within him—and implicitly inspired by the discovery of a poetic technique that could accurately convey that reality.

Viewing this period of his career in retrospect, Lowell commented, "I think I was a professional who was forced, who forced myself, into a revolutionary style in writing *Life Studies*, the biggest change in myself perhaps

I ever made or will." His revolution was twofold: shifting to an intensely personal subject matter, and finding a style perfectly suited to such subject matter—free enough to express the poet's "personal vibrance," yet subtly crafted, capable of giving the "vibrance" meaning and form. Of course, the sources of Lowell's achievement lay deep within his own creative imagination, but they were helped to flow by the example (and in some cases encouragement) of numerous other poets. Among these were Delmore Schwartz, Allen Ginsberg, Ezra Pound (the *Pisan Cantos*), D. H. Lawrence (his animal poems), Ford Madox Ford (*Buckshee*), and most importantly, Lowell's friend Elizabeth Bishop, his former student W. D. Snodgrass, and the poet he would come to call first among his "masters," William Carlos Williams.

Lowell's growing personal and artistic affinities with Williams during the 1950s made his *Life Studies* "revolution" possible. By 1950, what had begun in 1947 as a purely literary relationship had become a real friendship, marked by visits, compliments, and personal favors. Williams assumed his wonted role of master poet, alternately advising and reassuring Lowell, who in turn more and more assumed *his* wonted role of apprentice. Lowell needed help, and Williams alone among the modernist masters was willing and able to give it. Unlike Tate, Ransom, Eliot, Stevens, Frost, and Moore, Williams was emotionally warm and openhearted; and unlike Pound (who *was* warm and openhearted), he was relatively unegotistical. Even more important, Williams in the period following World War II continued to develop his art and his theories about art, and was eager to share his discoveries with all who might profit from them

For several seasons Lowell periodically visited Williams in Rutherford, bearing bottles of bourbon and set to "wallow in prosody." His poetry running dry, Lowell sensed that Williams's ideas of prosody spoke to his problem. After all, Williams's primary goal, as he wrote in "The Poem as a Field of Action" (1948), was a technique to "let our feelings through." On his side, Williams welcomed the younger poet's visits and told him that he hoped their talk would help to "dislodge us from our prejudices." But in 1950 Lowell decided to escape his dilemma by taking an extended tour of Europe with his new wife Elizabeth Hardwick. This was not so much a search for a fresh way of writing (as Williams had said of Auden's move to America), as a quest to renew the *old* way. Williams continued to advise and encourage Lowell in his private correspondence and in print.

When *The Mills of the Kavanaughs* appeared in 1951, Williams wrote an enthusiastic notice for the *New York Times Book Review*, but included hints of dissatisfaction with its form and feeling, qualities which both Williams and Lowell perceived as intimately connected. "When [Lowell] does under stress of emotion break through the monotony of the line, it never goes far, it is as though he had at last wakened to breathe freely again, you can feel the lines breathing, the poem rouses as though from a trance." Williams also questioned the narrowness of Lowell's "range of feeling." Despite such doubts, he conceded that "the rhymes are necessary to Lowell. He must, to his mind, appear to surmount them," and he generously summed up the volume as "excellent work. What can one wish more?" Yet Williams's stated reservations clearly indicated that he did wish something more: Lowell's liberation from self-imposed and perhaps now damaging, prosodic restraints.

In thanking him for the review, Lowell revealed that he shared something of Williams's hinted-at dissatisfaction. He had been reading Williams's recently published *Collected Later Poems* (1950), a volume brimming with vividly observed people, objects, and events. He was struck by the way the intricate, rich sentences, in a poem like "The Semblables," were given clarity and simplicity by being arranged in stanzas of short lines. "Reading over your volume," he wrote to Williams, "I've been wondering if my characters and plots aren't a bit trifling and cumbersome," somehow too remote from "what one lives." Clearly, even as *The Mills* was being published, Lowell had begun to consider Williams's poetry as a possible model, an alternative to such previous, and now exhausted, models as Tate and Eliot. Yet at this point, he was unable really to contemplate taking the leap to Williams's open forms: "But I'd feel as unhappy out of rime and meter as you would in them." A year later, still in Europe, he wrote that he wished "rather in vain" that he could absorb something of Williams's way of writing. Lowell was to spend the next five years preparing to absorb Williams, preparing to invent a poetry without regular meter or rhyme which would nevertheless satisfy his powerful yearning for form.

Lowell returned from Europe (as Williams had hoped he would) in 1953, spent a year teaching creative writing at the University of Iowa, a semester at the University of Cincinnati, and the remainder of the decade living on Marlborough Street in Boston and teaching at Boston University. During that time, Lowell and Williams continued to correspond and to pay each other visits. Their regard for each other grew. "Cal Lowell," Williams wrote to Pound, "is a man I respect and for whom I feel a strong bond of sympathy." He wrote to Lowell himself: "For spite of differences in our poetic styles I feel that we are close brothers under the skin." For his part, Lowell wrote to Williams upon hearing that he was ill, "I feel more love for you than for any man of your age."

Lowell's personal affection was paralleled by his growing artistic admiration. When *The Desert Music* appeared in 1954, he wrote Williams that "To Daphne and Virginia" and "Work in Progress" (a draft of "Asphodel, That Greeny Flower") were inexpressibly moving to him: "They are poetry and go beyond poetry." The book's advertisements quoted Lowell calling Williams "one of the best poets in the world." Lowell especially admired the brilliance and seeming ease of the poet's self-liberation from the modernist idea of the poem as impersonal object. In this last, great phase of his career, Williams's poems had become openly, movingly personal. They went "beyond poetry" to the emotional reality of life itself, closing the spaces between self, word and world. When *Journey to Love* appeared in 1955, containing the completed "Asphodel," Lowell wrote to Williams, "I've read *Journey to Love* many times. You are pouring out, and I know I shall be hearing your voice speaking the words to some inner ear in me, for as long—for as long as I journey myself."

Lowell's process of internalizing Williams's way of writing was boosted by two weekend visits from Williams, which coincided with speaking engagements at Wellesley in 1956 and Brandeis in June of 1957. At Wellesley, Williams read his recent poetry, ending with the Coda to "Asphodel." The audience, as he later remembered it, "practically carried me off on their shoulders. I was speechless." Seated in the audience, Robert Lowell was overwhelmed by Williams's reception and, even more, by the power of "Asphodel" itself. He wrote to Williams afterward to say that it was the best reading he had ever heard. In his essay "William Carlos Williams," Lowell vividly recalled the event: "It couldn't have been more crowded in the wide-galleried hall and I had to sit in the aisle. The poet appeared, one whole side partly paralyzed, his voice just audible, and here and there a word misread. No one stirred. In the silence he read his great poem 'Of Asphodel, That Greeny Flower,' a triumph of simple confession."

At Brandeis, Williams characteristically lectured on the rejection of traditional poetic forms, "the break from old arrangements of the words." His ideas must have seemed directly aimed at Lowell, sitting in the lecture hall.

> In this country is started, mainly, with Whitman. . . . He compared the past with the columns of a classic temple, that is to say the poems of the past, and the poems of the present to the waves of the sea: both have a certain metrical (or measured) regularity but the modern is far more flexible than the old. . . .
>
> [The contemporary poet] refuses to return to the past and yet doesn't quite know (he is alive and himself unexplained) where

to go for a new design with which to reaffirm the old life. He
will then proceed by instinct rather than to acknowledge defeat,
and write as he at least feels that he wants to do. Finally a
conscious design must evolve, all new, to be broken down later
into whatever the succeeding development out of chaos requires.

Williams concluded his speech by claiming that since Whitman, an important
development had occurred: the appearance of the "American Idiom" as a
unique modern language. The "American Idiom," Williams said, replaced
the "fixed standard foot" with a "variable foot," thereby restoring to measure
the dignity it had lost in modern times. As in his earlier essay "On Measure,"
he was suggesting that free verse need not be formless, but that its form
must result from the poem's organic, internal pressure rather than from
traditional patterns externally applied.

Lowell, obsessed as he was by the dialectic of freedom and form, wrote
afterwards to Williams that his speech "went to the heart," by which he may
have meant both the heart of the problem and his own emotional center. He
finally began to see a way out of his dilemma, a way to write unscanned
lines without relinquishing meaningful form—for, as Williams had said, "the
form IS the meaning (if it is a poem)." In the weeks immediately following
Williams's speech, Lowell began to write *Life Studies*, bolstered by Williams's
family chronicles, *In the Money* and the Preface to *The Dog and the Fever*.
Prosodically, Lowell did not specifically adopt Williams's own triadic stanza.
Rather, he took from him the idea of freedom: the idea that form is only
"*an* arrangement of the words for the effect, not *the* arrangement, fixed and
unalterable," the idea that if form is meaning then "the new form is the new
meaning."

On September 30, 1957, Lowell wrote to tell Williams that his artistic
block had been overcome:

> Your best work couldn't be more perfect and it has that life-blood
> of the arts, the real world. Well, we all get it in our different
> ways, according to our calling. I've been writing poems like a
> house afire, i.e. for me that means five in six weeks, fifty versions
> of each. I've been experimenting with mixing loose and free me-
> ters with strict. . . . I feel more and more technically indebted
> to you.

In December, after his first flood of inspiration had abated, he sent Williams
a packet of fifteen poems along with a note: "At forty I've written my first
unmeasured verse. . . . I've only tried it in a few of these poems, those that

are most personal. It's great to have no hurdle of rhyme and scansion between yourself and what you want to say most forcibly." Following this break-through, his letters to Williams all brim with feelings of admiration, grati-tude, and comradeship. (Soon after sending the poems, he wrote, "I have no master, only masters, you are about first among them." He was surely aware that a century before, Whitman had addressed Emerson as his "Master" in a note accompanying a packet of his poems.) Lowell pleased himself by thinking that he had "crossed the river" into Williams's world. After years of wishing in vain to absorb Williams's way of writing into his own, he had finally succeeded. Following a visit to his new mentor after *Life Studies* was finished but before its publication, Lowell wrote to him, "I'll go down to my grave in time thanking God that I have met Williams. . . . Ah, we are brothers."

Unlike Allen Tate, who was horrified by the manuscript of *Life Studies* and insisted that it not be published, Williams was frankly overwhelmed by Lowell's "terrible wonderful poems." When his wife Floss read to him aloud the packet of fifteen new poems (including "Skunk Hour"), he impulsively wrote to congratulate Lowell on his achievement: "You have opened a new field. You needed that break, rhyme could not contain you any longer, you have too much to say for that. . . . [This] brings one of my dreams for you into full fruit." Later when Floss read the completed manuscript of *Life Studies* to him, Williams wrote to Lowell, "You have piled accomplishment upon accomplishment until there is nothing to be said to you in rebuttal of your devastating statements or the way you have uttered them. . . . The book must have caused you some difficulty to write. There is no lying permitted to a man who writes that way." Williams, who was by 1958 rather infirm, broke the letter off here, resuming the following day with the ex-planation that he "couldn't go on" for the book had taken too much out of him.

At the risk of oversimplifying, we may say that Lowell absorbed three different but closely related lessons from Williams's poetry. The first was Williams's "variable foot," which he defined as "*relatively* stable" but not "rigid"—a relative measure to describe a relative universe. Williams (along with Charles Olson and Robert Creeley who helped him formulate his idea) was here returning to Emerson's theory of a poetry that is neither conven-tionally metered nor unmetered, but one in which the argument makes its own meter. For Williams, this idea became in practice the "triadic stanza," in which each line is a foot containing a variable number of syllables followed by an unrhymed pause:

> For our wedding, too
>   the light was wakened
>   and shone. The light!
> the light stood before us
>   waiting!
>   I thought the world
> stood still.
>   At the altar
>   so intent was I
> before my vows,
>   so moved by your presence
>   a girl so pale
> and ready to faint
>   that I pitied you
>   and wanted to protect you.
> As I think of it now,
>   after a lifetime,
>   it is as if
> a sweet-scented flower
>   were poised
>   and for me did open
>   ("Asphodel")

For Lowell, the idea resulted in a very different prosody, a line seemingly close to prose yet more rhythmical, and free to include rhymes and even passages of regular meter:

>   Oh my *Petite*,
> clearest of all God's creatures, still all air and nerve:
> you were in your twenties, and I
> once hand on glass
> and heart in mouth,
> outdrank the Rahvs in the heat
> of Greenwich Village, fainting at your feet—
> too boiled and shy
> and poker-faced to make a pass,
> while the shrill verve
> of your invective scorched the traditional South.
>
> Now twelve years later, you turn your back.
> Sleepless, you hold
> your pillow to your hollows like a child;

your old-fashioned tirade—
loving, rapid, merciless—
breaks like the Atlantic Ocean on my head.
("Man and Wife")

Lowell's line, like Williams's eliminates initial capitalization and regular rhyme and meter. It is, however, more proselike than Williams's, and at the same time more connected to traditional English prosody (the irregular rhymes, the underlying iambic rhythm). Lowell adapted his mentor's formal insights to suit his own particular needs. Williams in his essay "On Measure" had exhorted his followers to "invent new modes to take the place of those which are worn out," and Lowell's mode necessarily differed from Williams's own. But essentially their purposes were identical: to achieve a balance between freedom and order by basing the poetic line on a flexible "rhythmic unit" dictated by the poem's inner dynamic.

Secondly, Lowell adopted the "American Idiom" to replace the obscure, charged rhetoric of his earlier poems. The "American Idiom," which Williams thought must "shape the pattern" of the poem, entailed a rhythmic pace equivalent to the pace of speech and a diction akin to "the local American way of speaking." Williams's poetic language, as he told a hostile British questioner in an exchange recorded in his *Autobiography*, "came from the mouths of Polish mothers." Now Lowell sought a similar plainness of speech. Ignoring the seven types of ambiguity, Lowell in *Life Studies* deliberately aimed for "a tone that sounded a little like conversation." His new style was an Emersonian mixture of sophisticated diction ("my *Petite*, clearest of all God's creatures") and colloquial speech ("too boiled to make a pass"). In "My Last Afternoon with Uncle Devereux Winslow" Lowell typically varies "bibulous," "ingenu" and "Agrippina" the younger with such colloquialisms as "stogie" and "crummy," and with the clichés for which he has been criticized:

That's how I threw cold water
on my Mother and Father's
watery martini pipe dreams.

The voice speaking in *Life Studies* is that of Lowell himself, off his stilts. By his metrical experimentation and his emphasis on the language of common speech, he left what Edwin Fussell has called the "conservative" tradition of American poetic technique and moved toward Williams's own more "radical" tradition.

These technical lessons that Lowell learned from Williams directly relate to what is most important of all, the lesson he learned concerning content.

For Williams had stated plainly that the only real purpose of his stylistic innovations was to "liberate the possibilities of depicting reality in a modern world that has seen more if not felt more than in the past." Lowell used his new technical freedom to depict the reality of his own life history. He had, of course, been tempted by autobiography from the beginning of his writing career, but had lacked a poetics that would make undisguised autobiography possible. But now that he had developed a rhythm and language seeming to derive organically, even spontaneously, from his self, he could effectively confront his own authentic experience, and thereby return his poetry to its source.

In diminishing the space between himself as human being and himself as speaker of his poem, Lowell turned toward the poetic tradition of personal witness called for by Emerson in his essay "The Poet" and exemplified by such works as *Leaves of Grass*, the *Pisan Cantos*, and Williams's poems beginning with *Paterson*. In the poems of *The Desert Music* and *Journey to Love* in the mid-1950s, Williams relinquished his modernist pose of anonymity and objectivity and instead, in James Breslin's phrase, turned "increasingly inward, often into personal memory." In "Asphodel," Williams regales his wife with memories of their life together and assertions of abiding love, all as their "eyes fill / with tears." When Lowell called this poem "both poetry and beyond poetry" he was reiterating Whitman's point about *Leaves of Grass*: that it is more than a literary performance, it puts "*a Person* . . . freely, fully and truly on record." *Life Studies* in a similar way bridges the gap between poetry and life. Lowell said that the book was "about direct experience, and not symbols"; it tells his "personal story and memories." He called *Life Studies* "confessional" just as he called "Asphodel" a "confession." As is clearly shown by the contrasting passages of "Asphodel" and "Man and Wife" quoted above, Lowell's savagely ironic self-revelation differs tonally from Williams's confession, which radiates a sense of achieved wisdom and joy. Yet Lowell's poetry of the 1950s shares with Williams's the knowledge that "nothing can grow unless it taps into the soil." Williams once wrote to Lowell that he wanted to compose poems that would " 'say' what I am." Beginning with *Life Studies*, Lowell determined to do likewise (though in fact his poems more often say "what am I?").

Whereas Lowell's association with Allen Tate had once led him to adopt a style and viewpoint virtually synonymous with Tate's, his association with Williams led him to discover a style and viewpoint that were uniquely his own. Lowell the paleface donned the garb of the redskin, ceasing to think of art as discipline and beginning to think of it as a means of liberation. By precept and example, Williams persuaded Lowell finally to rebel against the authority of the past, English literary tradition, Boston, and his teachers at Kenyon. He persuaded Lowell to trust in the authority of the self. In his review of *Lord Weary's Castle* Jarrell had observed that Lowell's poems occupied a "kingdom of necessity" filled with "everything that is closed, turned inward, incestuous, that blinds or binds," but that "struggling within this like leaven" was "everything that is free or open, that grows or is willing to change." Jarrell called this latter impulse "accessibility to experience" and a "realm of freedom." Under the guidance of William Carlos Williams, Lowell in *Life Studies* departed from "the kingdom of necessity" and entered into "the realm of freedom." In 1952 Lowell had written Williams that he lacked Williams's "eye, experience and sense of language." In *Life Studies* he rediscovered his own eye and his own experience, and invented an appropriate language by which to convey them.

II

A second major influence on Lowell's development of a new style was W. D. Snodgrass. Snodgrass personally had little interest in Williams, but his poetry independently and concurrently reinforced the lessons Lowell derived from Williams. Lowell met Snodgrass in 1953 during his year teaching in the Creative Writing Program at the University of Iowa. A graduate student in one of Lowell's classes, Snodgrass himself was struggling under the confining orthodoxies of the academy, writing complex, erudite poems on themes remote from his own experience. Indeed, at this time the book he admired most and modeled his poetry upon was Lowell's own *Lord Weary's Castle*. But following a divorce, mental crisis, and a subsequent period of psychotherapy, he came to feel his poetry insincere and unfelt. The self, and the self's interactions with the world, began to seem the proper focus for poetry. Further influenced by the emotional intensity of Renaissance songs, Mahler's "Songs on the death of infants," and the straightforward poems of a fellow student named Robert Shelley, Snodgrass started to write poetry he later labeled "domestic" (rather than "confessional"), in a new unclotted style.

The entire movement of "Confessional poetry" may be said to have commenced on the evening of November 18, 1953, when during a piano concert Snodgrass scribbled on the back of his program lines which eventually became the beginning of "Heart's Needle":

> Child of my winter, born
> When the new soldiers died
> On the ice hills, when I was torn

The essentials of Confessional poetry are all present in these three lines: an undisguised exposure of painful personal event (in this case Snodgrass's divorce and separation from his child), a dialectic of private matter with public matter (the Korean War), and an intimate, unornamented style. The kind of writing Snodgrass initiated that evening would eventually come to include much of the best poetry in the 1950s and '60s: Snodgrass's own *Heart's Needle* (1959) and *After Experience* (1968), Lowell's *Life Studies* (1959) and much of his later work, Sexton's *To Bedlam and Part Way Back* (1960) and later volumes, Jarrell's *The Lost World* (1965), Plath's *Ariel* (1966), Berryman's *Dream Songs* (1969), and Kunitz's *The Testing Tree* (1971). (Ginsberg's *Kaddish* [1960], which certainly belongs to this group, might be said to have an independent line of origin.)

After leaving Iowa, Lowell continued his friendship with Snodgrass through correspondence and occasional meetings. At first Lowell seemed to disapprove of the new direction to Snodgrass's work, thinking it overly personal and sentimental. But by the time he began to write *Life Studies* (just after a selection of Snodgrass's poems appeared in the Hall-Pack-Simpson anthology *New Poets of England and America*), he had become an enthusiastic admirer of his former student. Writing to the poet Isabella Gardner, he called him the best of the younger poets. Viewing the matter in retrospect, Lowell told his *Paris Review* interviewer that Snodgrass "did these things before I did. . . . He may have influenced me though people have suggested the opposite."

Lowell had returned to Boston from the Midwest after his mother's death in 1954, apparently with the intention of writing about his family. *Time* quotes an anonymous friend as commenting, "The idea was to recapture some roots." Following an incapacitating manic-depressive episode, he began to work on a prose autobiography, but found prose "an awful job." He eventually broke off writing and published the completed fragment, entitled "91 Revere Street," in the *Partisan Review* in fall 1956. Although the proposed autobiography was aborted, the generative idea of making literary use of autobiographical material was not abandoned. Further, the experience of writing prose intensified his desire to write a poetry assimilating the language and cadences of prose. Prose seemed in many ways "better off than poetry" because "less cut off from life." Lowell had long admired the vitality of the prose passages in *Paterson* and had been newly impressed by the proselike qualities of Williams's and Snodgrass's most recent poetry. Now he began to think that "the best style for poetry was . . . something like the prose of Chekhov and Flaubert."

In March of 1957, Lowell went on a speaking tour of the west coast.

Reading his poems in San Francisco, in "the era and setting of Allen Gins-
berg," he was again struck by the insufficiencies of his poetic style: "I felt
my old poems hid what they were really about, and at times offered a stiff,
humorless and even impenetrable surface. . . . [They] seemed like prehistoric
monsters dragged down into the bog and death by their ponderous armor.
I was reciting what I no longer felt." Though "no convert to the 'beats,' "
Lowell did like "bits of Ginsberg" and thought *Howl*, like Snodgrass's poetry,
a breakthrough to "direct utterance." Ginsberg said that he had ceased to
make "a distinction between what you tell your friends and what you tell
your Muse."

Lowell returned from the West in April, attended Williams's Brandeis
lecture on the new measure in June, and left that same month with his family
for his annual summer stay in Castine, Maine. In Maine, his mind churned
with the new ideas he had encountered and with the new possibilities they
seemed to open up. He carefully read and reread Williams's family narratives
and also Elizabeth Bishop's personal yet coolly descriptive poems. Bishop
was a long-time friend of Lowell's, along with Jarrell the closest friend he
had. Moreover, Lowell admired her poetry more than that of any of his
other contemporaries. Rereading her poems, especially "The Armadillo," he
found yet another model for himself. The important aspects of Bishop's
poetry for Lowell were its open forms, conversational diction, precise de-
scriptions, and receptivity to human experience. Bishop's poetry, like that
of the Beats, was "exploratory" and "original"; unlike theirs, hers was
"controlled."

As early as his 1947 review of Bishop's *North & South*, Lowell had
associated her "bare objective language" with that of Williams. But Bishop,
possibly in contradistinction to Williams, was "one of the best craftsmen
alive." As Lowell's better craftsman, she seems to have made fully legitimate
for him the key elements of Williams's esthetics—the American Idiom, the
minute description yielding frequently to personal reflection, the scaled-
down, profoundly individual voice and vision. "You can see," Lowell later
told Stanley Kunitz, "that Bishop is a sort of bridge between Tate's formalism
and Williams' informal art." Using that bridge, Lowell crossed into a new
poetic world. "At times," he wrote to Williams, "I felt frightened of the
journey." Snodgrass and Ginsberg had lent impetus, and Bishop a sense of
legitimacy. But it was William Carlos Williams, through his encouragement,
ideas, and work, who had inspired Lowell to reinvent his art and hence
himself.

NEIL CORCORAN

Lowell Retiarius: *Towards* The Dolphin

Robert Lowell was never a decorous poet. Indeed, one of the few constants in his protean career is, precisely, an extraordinary and decided lack of decorum, a refusal of the conventionally proper and fitting. This indecorousness registers itself often, at the deepest possible level, as an apparently willed incongruity of form and feeling, of structure and content, of procedure and preoccupation. His infamous early Marian prayer—

> O Mother, I implore
> Your scorched, blue thunderbreasts of love to pour
> Buckets of blessings on my burning head—

achieves its terrible force exactly because it lacks all poetic propriety. ("Some of Lowell's early poems," said Berryman, in a perceptive oxymoron, "were savagely Marian.") The grotesquerie of the image, the thudding dilapidation of the rhythm, the sonorous obviousness of the delayed rhyme and gristly alliteration are an index of the depth of the human demand: feeling is expressed actually *through* the damage it does to the "poetry," and the reader is buffeted and elbowed out of the poem into the exacerbatedly febrile sensibility of the suffering man. Often in the early work, the intricate stanzaic patterning is wrenched out of shape, jolted out of rhythm or bellowed out of music by the sheer brute thrust of an energy and a need that call attention to themselves in ways perilously close to the meretriciousness and indulgence of bad poetry. In *Life Studies* the uncertain rhythms, the trailing lines, the flat tentativeness of the whole performance, as Lowell's words follow one

From *Agenda* 18, no. 3 (Autumn 1980). © 1980 by Neil Corcoran.

another with what John Bayley called "the crispness of cancellation," deliberately stretch the poems out beyond the page into their origin in a residue
of unverbalised actuality. At exactly the opposite pole, in *Near the Ocean*, the
calm measure of the Marvellian stanza, haunting our ears with the annihilating tranquillities of green thoughts in green shades, must cope with Lyndon Johnson "swimming nude, unbuttoned, sick / of his ghost-written
rhetoric," with "our monotonous sublime" in which there is "no true / tenderness, only restlessness, / excess, the hunger for success." The "delicious
solitude" of "The Garden" is invaded by an all too "rude" society.

These are instances of what I take to be fundamental in Lowell's work.
Its permanent air of risk, of recklessness and restlessness, its odd failures of
adjustment, emerge out of a thrust and impulsion deliberately to refuse the
polished or the finished and, in doing so, frequently to court disaster. The
work is always edgy, nervous, electric. Rejecting the stasis of lyric perfection,
Lowell's poetry kinetically involves and overwhelms us, and refuses to satisfy
or console in any of the ways the liberal tradition has taught us to expect of
great art. The lack of decorum and propriety I have described is the result
of something very close to an impatience with poetry itself, or at least with
the traditional certainties about the relationship between poetry and experience. Form in Lowell is not, in the end, as it was for Frost, a "momentary
stay against confusion," but an acceptance of it. Lowell's poems are everywhere bruised by the pressures of the exterior, the contingent, the unassimilated, the real, involved in "the lurch / for forms to harness Heraclitus'
stream." But they do "lurch" for form, however unsatisfactory they find it:
the alternatives of the merely random and aleatory are as insistently rejected
as the perfect adjustments of true decorum.

With the sequences of poems initiated by the first version of *Notebook*,
continuing through *History* and *For Lizzie and Harriet*, and culminating in
The Dolphin, Lowell's argument with form is carried to an ultimate point and
becomes, itself, a focus of thematic attention. The "sonnets" Lowell writes
in these sequences manage, in themselves, various kinds of impropriety.
Blank verse tending to corrupt into prose, and almost entirely unrhymed,
they are not really "sonnets" at all; and, in the "Afterthought" to *Notebook*,
Lowell actually celebrates his ability to write not-sonnets and fears that the
sequence as a whole fails quite "to avoid the themes and gigantism of the
sonnet." So why, we inevitably ask, write in a form that so insistently
summons to the eye and ear the extremely powerful ghosts of traditional
English lyricism? The answer can only be that Lowell *wants* us to be checked
and blocked by his "sonnets" in our legitimate expectations of what sonnet
form "ought" to do: Lowell's form is deliberately intended to leave us un-

satisfied and unfulfilled. He makes this, or something like it, explicit in a contemporary interview when he observes that he has attempted, in *Notebook*, to steal from the novel: it is essential, he says, that "poetry must escape from its glass." His "not-sonnets" or sub-sonnets might well be regarded as a collection of stones to hurl at this glass. But if this sort of thinking seems to fall neatly enough within a modernist provenance, *Notebook*, in its resolute and earnest presentation of a unified, coherent central personality and consciousness—presenting, evaluating, controlling, without any sleights of hand or ventriloquial invisibilities—seems an implicit affront to all our received notions of what a long poem can be like in the twentieth century. It asks to be taken as a quiet, but firm, rejection of what one would have thought Eliot had made magisterially axiomatic in *The Sacred Wood*, that "You cannot create a very large poem without introducing a more impersonal point of view, or splitting it up into various personalities." But the violences done in *Notebook* to sonnet form and to modernist "convention" may be thought justified in the book's extraordinarily intense presentation of the actual junctures between life and art. *Notebook* attempts to put its finger on the knot that ties experience to language, the public world of political action to the private self and its imagination. And the book catches Robert Lowell alive in flight, a spider living along the lines of his necessary and accidental relationships with history and with the difficult world beyond the self.

The problem, however, is complicated immensely by the subsequent recensions of the *Notebook* material. The revisions that set old lines in new contexts, old poems in slightly different forms, that sometimes give familiar poems an altogether different sense and context, seem devoted to emphasising the temporary, contingent nature of poetic form itself. Robert Lowell is not, of course, the only poet to revise himself in public, but these poems are so thoroughgoing an instance of the tendency as to make them different in kind from, say, Auden's self-revisions. And, further than any point Lowell's revisions make about poetry, they make a point also about the poetry market, about publicity, about status: the work that went into these revisions would have been pointless for any poet (i.e., almost every poet) who could not, like Lowell, make huge demands of his publisher. But, if these individual revisions seem to plead the primacy of the second thought, the third thought, the new juxtaposition, the alternative relationship—poetry as process, not realization—the eventual, "final" major forms Lowell finds in *For Lizzie and Harriet* and *History* seem to strive for more traditional clarities and coherences. *For Lizzie and Harriet* seems a step back towards the "themes and gigantism" of the sonnet sequence, dealing only with the domestic, familial and amatory material of *Notebook*. And Lowell would have us believe in his "Note" to

History that, by what he calls "plotting," he has, finally, "cut the waste marble from the figure." But the "plotting" in fact amounts to little more than having his poems proceed in chronological order, taking us from pre-history to the "end of a year" in which Lowell types his final, self-referential line—"bright sky, bright sky, carbon scarred with ciphers." Such plotting seems to me, as it has seemed to many of the book's critics, not a brilliant formal innovation in itself, and a manoeuvre that conveys an impression of form in conflict with material as profound as, but much more disturbing than, that of *Near the Ocean*. In that book the conflict releases, at its best, a terrible ironic force; but the idea of writing history as a sequence of sonnets has an acrobatic procrustean nonsense about it. It is almost as though Shakespeare had decided to handle the matter of his Histories as well as the story of his "two loves" in a sonnet sequence. The monotonous single-mindedness of the earlier poems in *History* is a reminder that even the "not-sonnet" has its strict limitations: to stray too far from the lyric impulse is to collapse the already tenuous form altogether. And the chronology of the sequence, intended presumable to do battle with the too obviously contingent, has the immense drawback of seeming to imply that the course of human history reaches its culmination and fulfilment in the life and works of Robert Lowell. The monotonous sublime is one thing, the egotistical quite another; and the faint whiff of the absurd and the hubristic about *History* makes it for me a much less compelling achievement than *Notebook*. The cutting of the marble from the figure seems altogether too wilfully perverse a performance.

But the lurch for form, and the drag away from form, become themselves centres of preoccupation in these sequences. Lowell is present in his *Notebook* poems as the writer writing. A characteristic procedure is the juxtaposition of an obviously "written" literary effect—the evocatively lyrical or the sonorously hieratic—with a reductive insistence on its resolute intendedness or on the mundane circumstances on which it depends. In "Through the Night" a marvellously precise and delicate little imagist poem (owing something to Pound's "In a Station of the Metro") is immediately smudged by Lowell's insistence on the contingency of his typewriter:

> The pale green leaves cling white to the lit night:
> this has been written, and eaten out on carbons.

The effect is, at the very least, to convey a weary impatience with his own talent. In "Onion Skin," the juxtaposition is the other way around, moving from an emphasis on the humdrum compunctions of the writer's job—in this case the use of a particular kind of typing paper made from particular trees—into a sudden clinching resolution in resonantly mythopoeic lines. The effect is, I think, the most spectacular in the whole of *Notebook*:

> This typing paper pulped in Bucksport, Maine,
> *onion skin*, only merchandised in Maine,
> creased when I pulled the last sheet, and seemed to scream,
> as if Fortuna bled in the white wood,
> first felt the bloody gash that brought me life.

Geoffrey Hill once observed that in Lowell's translations from Baudelaire's Jeanne Duval poems, the lyric "maintains a perilous autonomy against mundane attrition." In these *Notebook* poems, the autonomy is more perilous than ever, Lowell's conversation with himself and his argument with his own forms threatens a profound tonal disruption: some of these effects are almost equivalent to drawing a moustache on one's own Giaconda. But it is in the final of his sonnet sequences, *The Dolphin*, that this argument, I believe, reaches an ultimate resolution. As such, it brings to fulfilment not only these sequences, but an arc in Lowell's whole *oeuvre*: the book that followed it, *Day by Day*, is, significantly, all recapitulation, elegy and epilogue. I want to try to describe now the terms in which I think this resolution is accomplished.

The Dolphin is, of course, the book that is notoriously closest to the most potentially embarrassing circumstances of Lowell's private life—the final break from his long marriage to Elizabeth Hardwick and his new relationship with, and eventual marriage to, and child by, Caroline Blackwood. These circumstances—"one man, two women, the common novel plot"—provide the basic material of the sequence, as Lowell charts the course of his life through a crucial year, from one summer to another, in particular places (London, Oxford, hospital, the house *Milgate*, memories of America) and through letters and conversations. The pressure of the real is so acute that many of the book's reviewers (and Donald Hall again recently) have thought of it as a scandalous and embarrassing intrusion on marital privacies. It is something of a paradox then, though not—given the energies at work in Lowell's poems as I have described them here—a particularly surprising one, that *The Dolphin* also presents itself as Lowell's most obviously constructed, sustained and integrated poetic form. The individual poems in the sequence have an ease, assurance and fluency closer to traditional lyric utterance than anything in the earlier sequences; and the sequence as a whole makes use of a highly self-conscious coherence of patterned imagery associated with fishing and the underwater, and a central, radiantly inclusive symbol—the dolphin itself—which constantly suggest the ordering, controlling presence of the "shaping spirit of imagination": poetry, apparently, being set again firmly behind its glass. But the imagery and symbolism which Lowell discovers in *The Dolphin*, and the way he employs them, actually embody a sense of the tension between the present tense of his own existence and experience and traditional assumptions about the permanent form of art.

In his recent elegy for Lowell in *Field Work*, Seamus Heaney refers to him as "helmsman, netsman, *retiarius*." The last is actually Lowell's own word when he translates Baudelaire's "Le Voyage" in *Imitations*. In that poem, Time is the "retiare infame," a gladiator casting the weapon of his net to tangle and ensnare his victim. The combative relation to reality which Heaney's work implies is, I think, entirely just; but the image of the net is used in the first poem in *The Dolphin* to refer also to the combative, uneasy relationship Lowell has with his own art:

> The line must terminate.
> Yet my heart rises, I know I've gladdened a lifetime
> knotting, undoing a fishnet of tarred rope;
> the net will hang on the wall when the fish are eaten,
> nailed like illegible bronze to the futureless future.

In the book's final poem, *The Dolphin* itself is described as "this book, half fiction, / an eelnet made by man for the eel fighting." Between the two poems the book inhabits the two elements of air and water: the actualities, tangibilities and difficulties of Lowell's quotidian existence, and what he calls in "For the Union Dead" "the dark downward and vegetating kingdom / of the fish and reptile," the mysteriously resonant images which Lowell, as fisherman and "retiarius," draws into his net from a reservoir of submarine life. At its most reductive, and funniest, this strain of imagery situates a steaming Lowell in his bath-tub, willing himself into amphibiousness ("I soak, / examining and then examining, / what I really have against myself"). At its most serious, it discovers a sustaining, variable reticulation of metaphor, analogy and suggestion. In the nightmare poem "The Serpent," the fishing image suggests the poet as hierophant, taking his opportunity to transform the quotidian into the permanent, in the face of the inescapability of time, wherever in a human life chance and accident provide it:

> Like this, like this, as the great clock drags round,
> I see me—a green hunter who leaps from turn to turn,
> a new brass bugle slung on his invisible baldric;
> he is groping for trout in the private river,
> wherever it opens, wherever it happens to open.

This image of fishing contains and fulfils other such images of combative or aggressive relationship in the sequence—images of artist and model, of writer and plot, of actor and stage. It is an image of power and persuasion, but also of patience, endurance and waiting; and of the sudden moment of supreme, surpassing joy.

But the joy and tenderness of *The Dolphin*—a note, if not unique, certainly not sustained for any length of time in Lowell's previous work (the only really *tender* poems I can think of in the earlier work are those about Arthur Winslow, Lowell's grandfather, which all sustain a pathos of hurt and loss and a deep, grateful love)—emerge from Lowell's relationship with the central symbol of the dolphin itself. In the group of "Mermaid" poems, in which the women is seen, generally, in her more threatening aspect, the dolphin utters a crucial self-definition:

> I am a woman or I am a dolphin,
> the only animal man really loves,
> I spout the smarting waters of joy in your face—
> rough weather fish, who cuts your nets and chains.

As woman and dolphin, the symbol is announcing itself here as a deeply ambiguous one: the dolphin is loving and joyous, but the love and joy are made apparent in a gesture instinct with threat or, possibly, with taunt—"I spout the smarting waters of joy in your face"; and the cutting of nets and chains is, like the spouting of beneficent waters which cause the flesh to "smart" in withdrawing pain, an act of aggression before it is a releasing into new freedom. Both as woman and as poetic form, the symbol, throughout the sequence, *releases* exactly this sort of ambiguity: the dolphin threatens the dissolution of the ego, promises self-transcendence. In the one poem actually entitled "Angling," such transcendence is, for once, achieved and borne witness to: the fisherman is taken by his fish; the hunter is overcome by his prey; Jonah tumbles into the belly of the whale:

> I am waiting like an angler with patience and courage;
> the time to cast is now, and the mouth open,
> the huge smile, head and shoulders of the dolphin—
> I am swallowed up alive . . . I am.

This is the symbol's ultimate fulfilment. Lowell's being "swallowed up alive" is a triumphant self-realisation. The merging into the otherness of woman and of form is a "bright trouvaille," an unhoped-for release from the pressures of self-restriction, the containments of the ego.

The dolphin symbol here more or less announces its connection with the smilingly curved symbols of loving kindness and diligence in early Christian iconography; but two further significations also prompt attention. Lowell would certainly have known Elizabeth Bishop's poem "The Riverman" (which, in *Questions of Travel*, immediately follows "The Armadillo," an acknowledged influence on "Skunk Hour"). In this poem, the Dolphin is a water spirit with supernatural powers. The "riverman" of the title is an Amazonian peasant who wants to become a *"sacaca,"* a witch doctor drawing his power and authority from acquaintance with the water-spirits. The Dolphin described in the poem is masculine, but closely associated with the more numinous feminine spirit, Luandinha. The separation of the *"sacaca"* from his ordinary human family, because of his association with the river-spirits, is a central *motif* in the poem, and provides a note of pathos similar to that of Arnold's "Forsaken Merman" (and Lowell's regard for Arnold is, of course, also well catalogued). Miss Bishop's poem is, I think, at the very least, present to Lowell's imagination as a confirmation of his use of the dolphin symbol: the dolphin as all that threatens to separate Lowell as poet and man from more comfortable, familiar realities, but that also holds fascinating promise and numinous, awe-inspiring power.

But the symbol should also be seen, I believe, as itself finely reticulated in Lowell's own earlier works: it is a culmination, a final metamorphosis, of the steady procession of water-creatures and amphibians who swim and crawl through many of his poems—fish, of course, everywhere; but also, and especially, turtles and seals. In "Returning Turtle" from *Notebook*, Lowell takes a turtle which he has (rather oddly?) kept in his bathtub for a while, back to sea, and is allowed a moment of privileged witness:

> We drove to the Orland river, and watched the turtle
> rush for water like rushing into marriage,
> swimming his uncontaminated joy,
> lovely the flies that fed that sleazy surface,
> a turtle looking back at us, and blinking.

The irony of that final line, with its strategically placed comma, is a delicious one. The turtle might well look "back" at us; but we look a long way back at the prehistoric turtle. The blinking is, perhaps, a sly, wily expression of such distances and of the knowledge they give. It is a knowledge, anyway, which allows the turtle "uncontaminated joy," like the "preternatural" knowledge of seals in another *Notebook* poem where Lowell imagines "us" reincarnated as seals: "Creature could face creator in this suit, / fishers of fish not men." The dolphin inherits these uncontaminations. The man Robert Lowell suffers in the air of life—

> "your student wrote me, if he took a plane
> past Harvard, at any angle, at any height,
> he'd see a person missing, *Mr Robert Lowell*"—

to construct the fishnet of his book. The flashing fish are eaten, and the fishnet hangs on the wall, a stay against attrition carrying all its knots and ravellings with it—"nailed like illegible bronze on the futureless future."

In articulating the symbol of *The Dolphin* Lowell has, then, discovered a way of naturally and unforcedly suggesting, in the very tissue and texture of his poems, the sorts of relationship—between his life and his art, between the contingencies of the real and the stasis of the hieratic mode—which inform all his work. The symbol is a way of summoning, evoking and assuaging the need for form without denying the claims of the contingent. *The Dolphin* is a book that can accommodate an almost Beckettian dismissal of its own procedures—"I can't go on with this, the measure is gone" ("Tired Iron")—and a joyous celebration of what can be saved from the waters. It would be risking the sentimental to elaborate this further; but *The Dolphin* believes that the pains of the ego, the difficulties of the self, *can* be dissolved and assuaged in love and in art. But the poems themselves are never sentimental: they know, and admit, the cost. When the final poem in the sequence moves towards it climax in the overspill of a fifteenth line, Lowell is expressing a knowledge and a terrifying power, but also a guilt and an implicit plea for forgiveness:

> my eyes have seen what my hand did.

The guilt and the need for forgiveness are in the art as they are in the life; and the grandeur of *The Dolphin* is, as one of its poems has it of Yeats, a "grandeur of imperfection."

BRUCE MICHELSON

Randall Jarrell and Robert Lowell: The Making of Lord Weary's Castle

Randall was the only man I have ever met who could make other writers feel that their work was more important to him than his own. I don't mean that he was in the habit of saying to people he admired, "This is much better than anything I could do." Such confessions, though charming, cost little effort. What he did was to make others feel that their realizing themselves was as close to him as his own self-realization, and that he cared as much about making the nature and goodness of someone else's work understood as he cared about making his own understood. I have never known anyone who so connected what his friends wrote with their lives, or their lives with what they wrote.

—ROBERT LOWELL

In most of his published prose, Randall Jarrell presents himself not as a critic but rather as a reviewer, the distinction being anything but small. Jarrell's essays on poetry offer some remarkable insights; on the strengths and the limitations of the modernist movement, on the general shape and course of literature in this century, his observations match the wisest of his time. But because reviewing was the craft he commonly practised, his writing shaped itself to that craft, and a price of sorts had to be paid. Short was the space he could give to any one subject, and so he became famous for the quick, venomous strike, rather than for cooler, more patient, more precisely constructive criticism. Even Jarrell's admirers seem now to agree that when Jarrell came upon not another target but a truly gifted or at least a promising poet, he had a characteristic and disappointing response: "to name the names

From *Contemporary Literature* 26, no. 4 (Winter 1985). © 1985 by the Board of Regents of the University of Wisconsin System.

name the names of sustaining poems, to praise them with grateful adjectives."
Such a verdict is hard to appeal on the basis of Jarrell's published work. The
four volumes of essays convey the impression that Jarrell never got around
to playing that best of critical roles which he regularly exhorted his colleagues
to play, the role of the meticulous, passionate, yet circumspect helpmate,
working with quiet intensity to shape both the voices and the aesthetic that
the new age desperately needed but did not yet know how to demand. It
turns out, however, that this was not an unfulfilled promise in Jarrell's career,
but rather a case of his doing this kind of important work behind the scenes,
beyond the range of his essays.

In the Houghton Library at Harvard University there are more than
forty letters from Jarrell to Robert Lowell, including three that constitute
the surviving half of one decisive conversation between them at the close of
the Second World War. The tone of these letters suggests nothing of the
reviewer addressing the poet, either formally or off the record; Jarrell and
Lowell had been close friends for almost ten years, and the letters are alive
with the rapport these two young writers had come to share. But they also
show Jarrell playing the critic he himself called for, the critic in the highest
possible role, precise, circumspect, cautiously insistent; the letters prove that
Lord Weary's Castle, the volume of poems that made Robert Lowell a success
almost overnight, owes a heavy debt to the way Jarrell expressed himself
about the book in its formative stages. More, the letters show us a side of
Lowell that the biographies and the reminiscences commonly overlook, a
willingness on his part to listen carefully to advice—even to hear some serious
fault-finding—a willingness to go back to his poems, some of them already
much-revised, and change them yet again, turning flawed experiments into
works that would resound in American verse for the next three decades. At
the decisive moment, the competitive, notoriously volatile Robert Lowell
responded brilliantly to wise counsel, while the merciless reviewer met his
own challenge with sensitivity, wisdom, and above all tact, giving the right
sort of guidance in the right measure, truly helping, rather than flattering,
antagonizing, or otherwise confounding his difficult friend. Together Jarrell
and Lowell set American verse on a new course after the war; these letters
show how they managed to do it, the delicate way in which Jarrell kept
Robert Lowell on his precarious path toward the fulfillment of a great
promise.

In the autumn of 1945 Randall Jarrell was still on active duty in the
Army Air Force, but he had managed to keep his typewriter going through-
out the war, publishing regularly in *The Southern Review, Partisan Review,
The New Republic, The Nation*, the most influential literary journals of the

time. He had not only been writing reviews; since 1938, he had done far
more than his share in calling an end to the modernist era in American poetry
and in preparing readers for new movements and new stars. Much of what
Jarrell had published in the preceding seven years seems an odd balance of
elegy and impatience. In five extended articles he had set out to bury mod-
ernism in the tight box of a concise definition, enumerating its premises, its
patterns, its symptoms, tallying its achievements, addressing it always as
yesterday's romantic idea and today's exhausted convention. Each of these
essays has, as a kind of axis, a passage like the following, which could do
service either as an introduction to a retrospective anthology—of the sort
that Jarrell himself later edited—or as an unceremonious epitaph:

> The best of causes ruins as quickly as the worst; and the road to
> Limbo is paved with writers who have done everything—I am
> being sympathetic, not satiric—for the very best reasons. All this
> is a problem that disquiets most poets today; to write as good
> and plain a poem as you can, and to find it over the heads of
> most of your readers, is enough to make anyone cry. The typical
> solution of the twenties (modern poetry is necessarily obscure; if
> the reader can't get it, let him eat Browning) and the typical
> solution of the political poetry of the thirties (poetry must be
> made available to the People or it is decadent escapism; poetry
> is Public Speech—to use MacLeish's sickening phrase, so remi-
> niscent of the public prayer of the Pharisees) were inadequate
> simplicities, absurd half-truths. A classically rational and absurd
> solution is that of Winters and his school, whose willed and
> scrupulously limited talking-down has resulted in a kind of moral
> baby-talk. Auden's more appealing solution has worked out much
> better; it is too conscious, too thin, too merely rational: we should
> distrust it just as we distrust any Rational (or Rationalized)
> Method of Becoming a Saint. I am not going to try to tell the
> reader what the solution should be, but I can tell him where to
> find it: in the work of the next first-rate poet.

These were also years in which Jarrell was doing some of his fiercest
headhunting as a reviewer, dispatching one new poet after another as unfit
to take a place either in the current limbo, or even a small step beyond "The
End of the Line," as Jarrell titled his 1942 requiem for modernism. To be
sure, a similar edge of uneasy expectancy runs through almost everything
Jarrell wrote about poetry during the war years: Auden, the one truly in-
fluential poet still working, has grown too rational, lost his fire; the others,

Tate, Winters, Aiken, MacLeish, are all settling into comfortable, predictable moderation; the critics, who ought to be busy at the Arnoldian task of readying the world to appreciate the next first-rate poet when he appears, prove only how clever they are, and how reactionary, doing their "big-scale extensive criticism" when the time calls for intensive readings of individual poems. All the while, the university English departments remain their old unpromising selves, stuck in their deep-freeze of high Victorian taste. At the very close of one 1945 essay, however, Jarrell rises to uncommon buoyancy, in his praise for one slim volume from a very small press, a run of only two hundred and fifty copies. The book was Robert Lowell's *Land of Unlikeness*; and Jarrell's review of it does seem, as Ian Hamilton has observed, oddly disconnected from the poems which actually are included between its covers, and concerned much more with work that Lowell might soon do but had not yet managed. Jarrell's essay closes, in fact, with a comment that seems more an open exhortation to Lowell himself than an endorsement of the collection at hand:

> At his best Mr. Lowell is a serious, objective, and extraordinarily accomplished poet. He is a promising poet in this specific sense: some of the best poems of the next years ought to be written by him.

Jarrell's bright hope for a venture beyond modernism was someone he knew very well. Randall Jarrell and Robert Lowell had even shared a room while they were both students at Kenyon, each of them having been lured there in 1937 by the migration of Allen Tate and John Crowe Ransom northward from Vanderbilt. An experienced and dedicated student of Tate's, Jarrell had come to Kenyon as a Master's candidate; in the same year Lowell had astonished his Boston family by deserting Harvard—the only imaginable college for a genuine Lowell—after only two semesters and setting off to finish his undergraduate work with teachers he had read about, at what to a Brahmin sensibility must have been an unheard-of little college somewhere in the indefinite Midwest. Tate had introduced them to each other; Jarrell and Lowell became good friends, roommates, partners in the common cause of changing the fabric and direction of American verse. The friendship thrived as they went on their separate, even opposite ways; and by 1945, Jarrell the air-force officer and pilot-trainer was writing letters to Lowell, who had served a year as a draft resister, which contained statements like these:

> I haven't seen anybody I *know* in three years. You are the only writer I feel much in common with (when I read your poems I

not only wish I had written them but feel that mine in some
queer sense are related to them—i.e., if I didn't write the way I
do I might or would write the way you do; your poems about
the war are the only ones I like except my own—both of them
have the same core of sorrow and horror and so on) and the only
good friend of my own age that I have.

Towards the end of that year Lowell sent Jarrell the sheaf of poems
that Lowell intended to make into his first major book. The typescripts
included several poems from *Land of Unlikeness*, along with "The Quaker
Graveyard in Nantucket," which *Partisan Review* had published only re-
cently, and more than two dozen new poems. Jarrell responded with three
long letters on *Lord Weary's Castle*, as the book was tentatively called; two of
these letters go into great detail in their discussion of the poems. Jarrell
suggested all kinds of changes, from more punctuation to the adding and
dropping of stanzas, the deletion or complete overhaul of key lines, the
elimination of whole poems, the resurrection of others that Lowell had
intended to keep out of the volume. Jarrell also flooded many of the type-
scripts themselves with his marginal comments. What these papers offered,
in fact, is material for a long study of how *Lord Weary's Castle* actually came
about. But a briefer look at the most important changes that came about
under Jarrell's supervision reveals much not only about Lowell's creative
process, but about Jarrell's skill in rescuing Lowell from one near-disaster
after another.

Sorrow and horror: as Jarrell was well aware, these were at the core of
the sensibility that he and Robert Lowell shared as writers and as friends,
and exactly what both of them thought the postwar world required and
deserved from new poetry—but of course sorrow and horror can wreck a
poem at least as readily as they can express the spirit of the age. Lowell's
work from the very start of his career had shown an extraordinary urge to
face both private and public horrors head on; and his early poems had suffered
their fair share of damage from the effort. The essential drama of the poems
had been, from the outset, rebellion against not only his New England
ancestry and its moral, religious, and literary traditions, but also constantly
against himself, against even his own emotional excesses at other moments,
in other poems—to the extent of creating poems that by their closing lines
are casting scorn on the voice that began them. Over the course of the war,
Lowell had been writing new poems and rewriting older ones, changing
lines, adding and removing stanzas, combining shorter poems together and
taking longer ones apart. Jarrell saw the idea behind all this feverish changing

and adjusting: in a poetry not just about sorrow and horror but also about the indeterminate nature of the modern consciousness, the abiding uncertainty of any moral condition, the back-and-forth motions of the bewildered psyche, no small problem for a poet is the problem of making an end, finding some last words for any perception, any experience; and once finished, letting those last words stand. Lowell's obsessive perfectionism, in tandem with his unstable temperament, may have been leading him in the same general artistic direction that, for example, Yeats had followed, into a career whose hallmark would be constant change and revision; but during the early forties, Lowell's rewriting was as often to ill effect as to good. As a confidant, and as a critic perceptive enough to see the potential power of Lowell's taste both for extremes and for perfection, the possible good of venturing out to the frontiers of violent rejection, self-rejection, mystical terror, and bizarre consolation, Jarrell saw that his own role was to help Lowell express somehow a rage that did *not* tumble over into self-indulgence, childish petulance, preposterous distortions of common sense—or in the revisions and additions, retreat too far into rationality and complacency, too far away from the brink. "A characteristic of the immortals," Jarrell wrote later in an essay, is that "They oversay everything. It is only ordinary readers and writers who have ordinary common sense, who are able to feel about things what an ordinary sensible man should." This kind of odd praise is vintage Jarrell, and it encompasses its converse: that oversaying leads to hot air much more often than it does to the sublime. It is a testament to Jarrell's eye as a reader that he saw in Lowell the chance for the better fate, his susceptibility to the worse one; and that as someone Lowell trusted, Jarrell could take action to help Lowell make and maintain the essential distinction between the right and the wrong kind of excess, the right and wrong kind of restraint.

On the ending Jarrell's letters focus most regularly, and here he had his most important effect on *Lord Weary's Castle*. A dramatic example of that influence is the saving change that took place in one of the best poems in the collection, "Mr. Edwards and the Spider," which was a new work when Lowell sent it to Jarrell, having not appeared in any from in *Land of Unlikeness*. Perhaps the handsomest achievement in "Mr. Edwards" is its carefully balanced, compressed portrayal of three different sides of Jonathan Edwards's complex personality, his calm, scientific detachment in observing the natural world; his genius and courage in applying what he found there to the teachings of Scripture; and the steadiness with which he could look into horror and speak its essence to multitudes and generations. Further, because it manages to represent several aspects of one extraordinarily full consciousness, the poem compounds in its implications. Lowell's complete Jonathan Ed-

wards ultimately speaks not only an eighteenth-century mind, but a much
more modern sensibility as well—detached, scientific, historical, horrified,
all at the same time. But the poem Lowell sent to Jarrell in Texas has nothing
of this reach and resonance; the trouble lay precisely in the way the poem
ended. In the last lines of the typescript, the spider

> stretches out its feet
> And dies. Insect, this is the soul's defeat;
> No strength exerted to oppose the heat
> Then sinews your abolished will. The soul,
> Burning Black Widow, cinders in a bright coal.

Only one side of Edwards speaks in these verses; the terrifying evangelist
of "Sinners in the Hands of an Angry God" drowns out both the naturalist
and the careful, deliberate theologian. This fire-and-brimstone version of
Edwards, moreover, has gone too far into panic, too far away from reflection:
for the rhetoric and the sensations evoked here are so strong that thought at
last is driven out of the poem, and the previous meditations are not completed
but overwhelmed. Jarrell's counsel about this poem is a good indication of
his general strategy in working with Lowell, with both the verse and the
man behind it. Avoiding scholar-critic homilies to his friend about abortive
themes or lost opportunities of some general kind, Jarrell responds strictly
to the problems of language and meter in the closing lines. He leads Lowell
back to consider the whole ending as a failure of craftsmanship, and thereby
to discover for himself how much more the poem could do. Jarrell's comment
at the bottom of the typescript is focused and terse:

> Rhythm awkward. You generally have one line in a poem when
> the rhythm gets not just harsh but gets tetanic like a muscle under
> too long tension. Also, *burning, Black, cinders,* and *bright coal* are
> too much fire and its effects for one line.

Not in itself very surprising or profound, this remark comes in tandem
with an observation on a much different scale, in the final pages of the
accompanying letter. There Jarrell penetrates to the deeper and broader
problem behind "Mr. Edwards" as it then stood, the trouble underlying the
awkward rhythms and overdone rhetorical effects:

> I think you're potentially a better poet than anybody writing in
> English. I think your biggest limitations right now are (1) not
> putting enough about *people* in the poems—they are more about
> the actions of you, God, the sea, and cemeteries than they are

about the "actions of men"; (2) being too harsh and severe—but this already changing, very much for the better too, I think. Contemporary satires (which you don't seem to write anymore) are your weakest sort of poem, and are not really worth wasting your time on; your worst tendency is to do too-mannered, mechanical, wonderfully-contrived exercise poems; but these you don't do much when you feel enough about the subject or start from a real point of departure in contemporary real life.

These are no judgments that Jarrell ever leveled in print at Lowell's poetry, early or late; they are confidences, offered at a time when, as Peter Taylor remembers about those years, "Cal was *determined to learn what he could from Randall*" [emphasis Taylor's]; and such an enumeration would certainly make a disciple take notice. The proof lies in what happened to "Mr. Edwards," which was suffering precisely from too much harshness and severity, too much of Robert Lowell performing and too little of anything else. Rewriting the ending of the poem, Lowell altered the last four lines for an entirely different effect, and appended a whole new closing stanza. The rhythm-changes that Jarrell called for contribute much more than a gentler cadence in the ear: the poem now moves from quiescent observation into passionate, prophetic insight, then onward into a final mood that suggests not unending panic, but rather a kind of peace, of the sort that comes of knowing the completeness and the truth of one's own perceptions. The calm of the new ending is more chilling than the flamboyant terror that it replaced. Edwards now conceives the human condition with all sides of his balanced and wide-ranging consciousness, as the naturalist and the theologian as well as the shocker of congregations:

> This is the sinner's last retreat;
> Yes, and no strength exerted on the heat
> Then sinews the abolished will, when sick
> And full of burning, it will whistle on a brick.
>
> But who can plumb the sinking of that soul?
> Josiah Hawley, picture yourself cast
>   Into a brick-kiln where the blast
>   Fans your quick vitals to a coal—
>   If measured by a glass,
> How long would it seem burning! Let there pass
> A minute, ten, ten trillion; but the blaze
> Is infinite, eternal: this is death,
> To die and know it. This is the Black Widow, death.

It is startling to find here now, of all things, a faint echo of Whitman's "Out of the Cradle Endlessly Rocking"—the resonance is bizarre, incongruous, and perfect at the same time. *Death* like a repeated mantra, the slowing of the meter, the evocation of the "Black Widow," here calling up a stately, even a pathetic human form as well as the menace of the most deadly American spider, all convey the only kind of peace that Lowell's Jonathan Edwards—not merely Lowell himself—can find in comprehending what it means to be dead and damned: the peace that comes of knowing the whole truth, of not being rocked into error by pretty lies or the soft sound of a name. The poem has regained not only its composure but also those other voices of Edwards's that have spoken out earlier. The new ending pays genuine homage to Edwards, draws him forward, morally, into our own time, and establishes a valid kinship of mind between Edwards and Robert Lowell; conversely, it is a showpiece for Lowell himself, demonstrating that he has that same capacity for grace and calm in his own most perilous moments, and for truly understanding a mind beyond himself, an experience beyond his own.

The companion-piece to "Mr. Edwards and the Spider" lay in equally serious trouble when Lowell sent it to Jarrell for his reactions. In the case of "An Eighteenth Century Epistle"—which eventually became "After the Surprising Conversions" in *Lord Weary's Castle*—the heart of the problem was much the same. Also a new poem, it is based upon a letter from Edwards to Benjamin Colman in 1735, at a time full of both promise and darkness for Edwards. The Great Awakening that Edwards had fathered and seen grow so far beyond reasonable hopes had been recently stunned by the suicide of Edwards's own close relation, the same Josiah Hawley addressed in the spider poem. The letter is rich ore for a dramatic monologue, full as it is with both hope and anxiety. Edwards is exhilarated by the rise of religious fervor, frightened by despair and self-slaughter in his own family, and by those "other appearances," as the original letter calls them, "of Satan's rage amongst us poor souls." The artistic challenge to the poet is that this letter offers Edwards at both high tide and low ebb; a poem that sought to catch even half of this mood must still make it uniquely and recognizably Edwards's, rather than, say, Cotton Mather's—or even Robert Lowell's, speaking through some thin, unconvincing Edwards mask. What such a poem could be—what of course it eventually became—is another dramatic monologue with that rare gift of speaking with several voices, and more, with the mature voice of the poet as well. The very creation of such a poem says much about what it is to live with both doubt and hope, to seek to express them as one coherent utterance, to live with a divided self and still strive to be whole. Lowell had a large stake in such a poem: even at this early time in his career, he had written, in verse, many of his own sermons, was in effect trying to stir up his own Great Awakening in American poetics and to face and express the great destructive forces loose in the world. The poem was a chance to address not only darkness but the question of how, or even whether, one could continue to write poetry, with such sorrow and horror all around.

In the typescript Lowell sent to Texas, the original ending seems so flat, so defeated, that one wonders how either this implausible Jonathan Edwards, or the Robert Lowell who conceived him, could ever go on to any other enterprise, preach another sermon, write another line:

> God
> Abandoned us to Satan, and he pressed
> Us hard, until we thought we would not rest
> Till we had done as that mad fool had done;
> All the good work is quashed. We are undone.
> The breath of God has carried out a planned
> And sensible withdrawal from this land;
> The multitude, once unconcerned with doubt,
> Once neither callous, curious, nor devout,
> Starts at broad noon, as though some peddler whined
> At it in its familiar twang: "My friend,
> Come, come, my generous friend, cut your throat. Now;
> 'Tis a good opportunity. Now! Now!"

Jarrell's reaction to all this is to bear down, as he regularly does in these letters, on metrics and specific word choices:

> This rhythm seems pretty awful. The *idea* of having it just like the peddler's invitation is good, but I don't think you've really made up a good peddler's motivation, either in rhythm or words. If a peddler went arounding [*sic*] saying *'Tis a good opportunity* he would starve to death—that isn't really as urgent and impressing as he'd make his sales-talk. And though the *Now! Now!* might work, probably would, if you fixed up the rest of the speech, it doesn't now. I think the rhythmical effect "my generous friend, cut your throat" (where I've underlined) hurts particularly. I don't imagine it would be very hard to change the peddler's speech a little.

Jarrell casts a decisive doubt here, for his comment implicitly questions whether there really can be any "good peddler's motivation" for a speech like this at the end of such a poem, no matter what language that speech might be couched in. True to his general conception of Lowell's strengths and shortcomings, Jarrell is again coaxing his friend to create a real rather than an abstract, hypothetical voice, and to recognize that the ending, as it then stood, failed not only in its language and its meter but also in its basic credibility. It goes without saying that Edwards would never close an epistle or even a private meditation in such a state, and that the poem, by failing to keep faith with its own persona or to find any way around this opportunity to become another suicidal "mad fool," cuts its own throat thematically. Lowell's subsequent reworking of the poem's conclusion may seem modest, compared to what he did with "Mr. Edwards and the Spider": here he alters a few verb tenses and adds three more lines beyond the "Now! Now!"—lines that are literally off the subject. But simply by putting the Hawley catastrophe in the past tense, Lowell can grant Edwards—and himself in the bargain—some measure of escape from absolute despair; and the apparently random perceptions in the new ending, a letter's idle talk about September, draw the reader back for a closer look at the season mentioned in the very first line—to ponder the strangeness in the bounty of early autumn. The closing three verses affirm the richness and the promise of life even as they seem to tremble at so much waste:

> Content was gone.
> All the good work was quashed. We were undone.
> The breath of God had carried out a planned
> And sensible withdrawal from this land;
> The multitude, once unconcerned with doubt,
> Once neither callous, curious nor devout,
> Jumped at broad noon, as though some peddler groaned
> At it in its familiar twang: "My friend,
> Cut your own throat. Cut your own throat. Now! Now!"
> September twenty-second, Sir, the bough
> Cracks with the unpicked apples, and at dawn
> The small-mouth bass breaks water, gorged with spawn.

Will these apples of opportunity be picked, or will they fall in a neglected orchard? Will the "gorged" bass replenish the depleted autumn streams of New England, or is it glutting itself on the young? The mysteriousness of Lowell's new ending not only better fits the spirit of the original letter; it saves him from one of those blind alleys of certainty that could make his voice intolerable, and further poetry in a sense impossible. These overloaded limbs and gorged fish are gorged with a possibility of more poems as well; for Lowell has now brought both Edwards and himself away from the peddler's sinister call.

For years, however, both the poet and his critic of choice had understood that Lowell's special challenge lay in writing about matters closer to home. Lowell's great subject of course is his own family, his personal history, his own various identities; he was compelled to pass judgment upon his upbringing and his private world and to translate that world into poems of consequence. The dangers of such an undertaking come easily to mind, among them the risk of high-handed scorn, or equally high-handed forgiveness. Those poems in *Lord Weary's Castle* that are most "in the family," most suggestive of the "confessional" phase of his career that *Life Studies* would announce a decade later, are the three poems on his Winslow relations: the four sonnets borrowed from *Land of Unlikeness* in memory of Arthur Winslow, the new poem "Mary Winslow" (titled "Forest Hills Cemetery" in the typescripts), and the new poem "Winter in Dunbarton," an attempt at an elegy in the family churchyard. Lowell had been working on the set, especially on the Arthur Winslow poems, in the months since *Land of Unlikeness* had appeared, and in the process he had apparently numbed his own sense of what kind of tone was needed to sustain them, make them comprehensible and significant to anyone beyond himself. "Death from Cancer," the first poem of the series "In Memory of Arthur Winslow," had lost its half-ironic, half-mystical closing; tinkering with the final five lines, Lowell had come up with this revision:

> and your ghost
> Twitters and flits until the Oarsman run
> Arthur upon the trumpeting black swan
> Beyond Charles River to Acheron
> Where the wide waters and the voyager are one.

And this alternative:

> And like a figure-head
> You cup your hands. When will Our Lady bear
> Arthur upon her trumpeting black swan
> Beyond Charles River and the Acheron
> Where the belled waters hold the kneeling voyager?

Jarrell responded more bluntly to these changes than to anything else in the packet:

The most important part of the letter now arrives: please, please, for goodness sake change A. W. I, *Death From Cancer* back to what it used to be. The old ending was one of the best—and the most genuinely mysterious, magical, haunting, good-beyond-explanation endings you've ever done; the new ending seems a perfectly good mural in a church, but not a bit more: it's good fairly conventional religious poetry, and the old was *wonderful*. I actually believe in the quiet; with the second I just suspend my disbelief indifferently. . . .

But the important thing is the ending. I think it's harder for the poet to recognize a "magical" effect than it is for the reader, and the poet may prefer the well-constructed sensible one he builds up to take its place. You compare both of them and see if you don't feel that way about the two endings.

Lowell did as he was counseled; the extra stanza was dropped, and the poem appeared in *Lord Weary's Castle* with only one word changed from its previously published form. The will to be serenely meditative had led Lowell similarly astray in "Forest Hills Cemetery," a dark, unsettling elegy about one of his great aunts. In its typescript form, this poem too had grown one stanza too many: of the three, it is the second that works the best, fading eerily from faint life into the obscure promise of death:

> But stop,
> Neighbor, these pillows prop
> Her that her terrified and child's cold eyes
> Glass what they're not: our Copley ancestress,
> Grandiloquent, square-jowled and worldly wise,
> A Cleopatra in her housewife's dress;
> Nothing will go again. The bells cry: "Come,
> Come home," the babbling Chapel belfry cries:
> "Come, Mary Winslow, come; I bell thee home."

Lowell's attempt to expand on this astonishing moment had led him only into a kind of stasis—unfruitful references to family history, a tritely expressed hope for a Glorious Resurrection, a closing atmosphere of dry, unevocative uncertainty:

> Pomp and the winds of dogma will not grate
> Your bowels, Mary, on that last estate
> Beside my Uncle Devereux, your loved son,
> A graced man and a father, run

> To earth when he was thirty-one
> Under his huge, unhandy granite cross,
> Free in an alien and suburban ground
> Until the trumpet sound
> Resumption to the soul and body. Moss
> Drags at the trees and head-stones, but the air
> Moves only as it tries the daffodils
> Thwacking about your ears in Forest Hills;
> And the unruly, casual elms bestir
> The dog-tired whip-poor-wills.

Jarrell's reaction, running down the right-hand side of the manuscript, is brisk and direct:

> I think you ought to leave out this stanza, which is *very* flat and scrappy compared to the other two, more like an after thought [*sic*]. The first two stanzas make a much better poem by themselves. I'm almost certain this is correct. Look at the 3rd stanza skeptically and see how little it resolves or completes or carries to a higher level the first two. The end of the 2nd stanza makes a beautiful end for a poem. I like the two stanzas as a complete poem very much.

He drives the point home in one of the letters:

> I think the first two stanzas of *Forest Hills Cemetery* make a good poem by themselves, and are hurt a lot by the last stanza which is a little too personal-reference à la Yeats—you expect her to turn out to be Lady Gregory's sister-in-law.

The extra stanza accordingly went the way of Lowell's misguided expansion of "Death from Cancer." Falling between them, in the sequence of *Lord Weary's Castle*, is "Winter in Dunbarton," a center panel in an unsettling triptych of family ghosts. Ultimately a meditation on the Lowell burying ground near Boston, the poem, which had not appeared before, dwells for half it's length on, of all things, a dead family cat, and turns only at the last possible moment to Dunbarton and Lowell's ancestors. The theme immanent in the published version warrants the risk that Lowell takes in such an oblique approach to his subject, the final leveling of pet cats and famous men to the same end beneath the cracking, untended monuments. The version that Jarrell first read, however, had gone far over the edge into perversity and sensationalism. The cat of this earlier "Dunbarton" is not quite dead—and, consequently, it is in the beginning now that the poem fails in taste, in tonal control, in continuity with the rest of it:

> Time smiling on this sundial of a world
> Corrupted the snow-monster and the worm
> Ransacking the shard statues of the peers
> Of Europe, but our runted cat lies curled
> For rigor mortis. Her wet breathing smears
> My fingers; worms in yellow acid squirm
> Over her matted whiskers and her ears.

Jarrell's comment on the typescript:

> This is a little too much, laid on so thick that the reader feels, consciously or unconsciously, that you're trying to make him sick. You ought to make *some* detail a little milder—I could do without the worms—or *something*. This isn't my cat-loving but my poem-loving self talking, incidentally.

The major changes Lowell consequently made in this first stanza not only do away with the gratuitous details and the implicit voyeurism; Lowell hits upon a conceit to tie the whole poem together much more tightly and poignantly. All the sick humidity and luridness is replaced with sheer cold, as the essential kinesthetic experience of death:

> Time smiling on this sundial of a world
> Sweltered about the snowman and the worm,
> Sacker of painted idols and the peers
> Of Europe; but my cat is cold, is curled
> Tight as a boulder: she no longer smears
> Her catnip mouse from Christmas, for the germ—
> Mindless and ice, a world against our world—
> Has tamped her round of brains into her ears.

In keeping with the much-changed atmosphere of this new opening, Lowell pours ice into the final stanza as well. While the typescript reads:

> and the dead
> Narrow and narrow in the thankless ground
> Grandfather wrenched from Charlie Start and sold
> To the selectment [*sic*] of Dunbarton. Head
> And shoulders narrow;

the published version becomes:

> and the dead
> Chatters to nothing in the thankless ground
> His father screwed from Charlie Stark and sold
> To the selectmen. Cold has cramped his head
> Against his heart.

Lowell hits upon a genuine continuity now with the climate that dom-
inates the companion-piece poems in the Winslow set: the "cold sun" and
the autumnal pine cones on Arthur's casket, the "rigid Charles, in snow,"
that serves as the frozen axis for the world of Mary Winslow, who looks out
over that world one last time with "a child's cold eyes." The Dunbarton
cemetery, as the final home of the Lowells, a home evoked strikingly now
in the recurring presence of the cold, lifeless cat, becomes the vanishing
point toward which cats and Winslows and Lowells must all converge. Thus
transformed, the poem itself works as a kind of vortex, drawing toward itself
those disorienting, converging motifs of the other two elegies in the set,
motifs that sweep those elegies towards their own respective enigmas. The
"Arthur Winslow" that Jarrell helped save does not end so much as disappear
over a brink:

> and the ghost
> Of risen Jesus walks the waves to run
> Arthur upon a trumpeting black swan
> Beyond Charles River to the Acheron
> Where the wide waters and their voyager are one.

Similarly, the "home" towards which the Chapel belfry tolls Mary
Winslow gains extra shading from "Dunbarton"; coming just after, "Mary
Winslow" seems to move not merely outward and away from human com-
prehending, but toward the central mystery of the elegy before. Not a word
suggesting any such arrangement turns up in Jarrell's letters or marginal
notations. Jarrell never tried to write Lowell's poetry for Lowell; as a friend,
as a confidant, and as an influential reviewer, he knew exactly what he could
and could not legitimately do in coaxing Lowell's talents toward their own
fruition. Jarrell confined himself unfailingly to gentle but well-aimed prov-
ocation, giving his friend a good sense of what was specifically and unar-
guably amiss in particular poems, and a general notion of what possibilities
were yet to be explored. There is no question that Jarrell recognized what
promise lay in the poems that Lowell had entrusted to him, or the importance
of his own response, not only for Lowell but also for the future of American
poetry. He tells Lowell as much in one of the letters:

I think it's terribly important for you to get your book absolutely perfect . . . for this reason: it will be the best first book of poems since Auden's *Poems*, and might, with luck or sense on the people's part, be a wonderful success. . . . I think they are some of the best poems anybody has written in our time, and are sure to be read for hundreds of years. I am *sure* of this: I would bet hundreds of dollars on it.

One way or another, the absolute perfection had to be Robert Lowell's, not Randall Jarrell's; comparing this private tact and self-restraint with Jarrell's famous savagery in print, one begins to appreciate the kind of balance he managed to keep up in his efforts to help his friend. "Christmas Eve under Hooker's Statue," which had appeared as "Christmas Eve in Time of War" in *Land of Unlikeness*, is another case in point, another poem that had gone astray in the revision. Since *Land of Unlikeness*, Lowell had reduced the poem by eighteen lines, two full stanzas, and had sharpened its details and perceptions considerably—the abstract "Civil War Monument" has become the statue of General Hooker, someone who can be directly addressed, even blamed in part for America's political and moral troubles; and Lowell's rage at the ongoing slaughter is no longer thrown off course by petty complaints about price controls. The final stanza of the *Land of Unlikeness* poem could not decide what to complain about: wars of any and every description, the souring of a just cause by greed, or this particular war as instigated by the rich. Some of these lines could even be read as a celebration of war as a way for materialists to destroy themselves:

> Stone men at war,
> Give me the garish summer of your bed—
> Flaring poinsettia, sweet william, larkspur
> And black-eyed susan with her frizzled head:
> My child is dead upon the field of honor:
> His blood has made the golden idol glimmer.
> "I bring no peace, I bring the sword," Christ said,
> "My nakedness was fingered and defiled."
> But woe unto the rich that are with child.

Replacing this shapeless bitterness, Lowell had written a new final stanza for the poem he sent to Jarrell, but Jarrell was not encouraging in his marginal comments: "Much better than the old; you've left out most of the bad things, but I don't believe it's a good poem yet." The accompanying letter advised Lowell to leave "Christmas Eve" out of the book entirely. Jarrell objected particularly, in his marginal notes, to the vague use of "the elder" in the new seventh line, to the awkwardness and sheer inaccuracy of a quotation in the eighth, and to the closing verse, simply as a finish he did not "much like":

> His stocking is full of stones. Fragile and red,
> The Statehouse stares at Hooker. Man of war,
> Where is the garish pathos of your bed,
> Flaring poinsettia, sweet william, larkspur
> And black-eyed susan with her frizzled head:
> The victims dead upon the field of honor?
> "I bring no peace but swords," the elder said,
> "My nakedness was handled and defiled,
> But woe unto Jerusalem got with child."

The heart of the problem is that the images here seem almost random, unconnected in every important sense from the preceding stanzas. The time remains Christmas, yet the poem jumps to a closing with spring flowers, to Jerusalem as the Easter City; if there is an irony or a seasonal transition intended here, it has not begun to be realized on the page. Hooker too, a strong presence in the first and second stanzas, is simply dropped and forgotten. Compare these lines with those Lowell subsequently found to replace them, lines that instead tie the poem together, turning back to Hooker now as the "blundering butcher" in his famous defeat at Chancellorsville, to the season of Christmas, to the resonating image in the first stanza of a small boy reaching into the Christmas stocking and finding "hell's serpent" coiled around "the apple in the toe." The final line of the transformed poem is another breakthrough, in both mood and coherence, for now Christ's final appearance echoes Lowell's opening memories of a childhood Christmas, his adult sense of loss, and the cultural errancy and confusion that are a strong theme in the rest of the poem. More, Lowell replaces Christ's words with those of a fellow New Englander, someone to converse with about the Hooker legacy—now much more sharply defined, as the old delusion that war is glorious, innocent, holy enterprise:

> Santa in red
> Is crowned with wizened berries. Man of war,
> Where is the summer's garden? In its bed
> The ancient speckled serpent will appear,
> And black-eyed susan with her frizzled head.
> When Chancellorsville mowed down the volunteer,

"All wars are boyish," Herman Melville said;
But we are old, our fields are running wild:
Till Christ again turn wanderer and child.

Of the half dozen other poems Jarrell offered some detailed advice on, four underwent minor changes at his suggestion: a new penultimate line for "Christmas in Black Rock" (a new poem which was called "All Souls in Black Rock" in typescript), two changed metaphors and a repair to the meter in the last stanza of "The Dead in Europe," a line substitution in "The Exile's Return," different closing verses for both of the typescript versions of "At a Bible House," both of which were also new, and neither of which Jarrell voiced any enthusiasm for as worthy of the book. Lowell had also sent along two versions of "At the Indian Killer's Grave," large portions of which had been borrowed from "Cistercians in Germany" in *Land of Unlikeness*; one of these versions was considerably shorter than the other; in a series of marginal comments Jarrell made his case for the greater clarity and impact of the longer poem—the one that Lowell selected for *Lord Weary's Castle*. The letters also indicate that Jarrell's opinions had much to do with which poems were left out of the book and which others might be salvaged from *Land of Unlikeness*. One of the letters offers summary opinions on what Lowell should and should not include—and the table of contents that resulted shows very little quarrel with Jarrell's opinions:

> I agree about all the others you're using from your first book; it's the same list I would make, except I'd put in *Christ for Sale* too. (Though certainly most of your readers won't like *it*.)
> The only one of the new bunch of sonnets I like is *The Soldiers*. If I were you I'd not use the others (*Pentecost, Midas, Babel, The Benedictines*) in this book, but let them lie around a while and see what you want to do with them.

"The Soldiers" appears in *Lord Weary's Castle*; the other sonnets do not. Nor does "Christ for Sale," Jarrell's caution perhaps having something to do with convincing Lowell not to take the chance of putting it in. Even so, it does not seem that any of this eliminated "new bunch" was a poem that would make or break even a slim volume. None of them was the sort of *tour de force* in which the poet grapples with his most difficult, most consequential symbols, his most complex and urgent ideas—about the world, about himself, about poetry itself as a mediating force between the two.

That special challenge is taken up in *Lord Weary's Castle* by "The Quaker Graveyard in Nantucket," the central metaphors of which—the sea, the white whale, the legions of dead sailors, the Virgin, the final rainbow of God's mysterious covenant with man—all announce it as a poem that is trying to do everything, aiming at nothing short of an expression of man's fate, his place in nature and in the eyes of God, the meaning of New England history, the moral core of its literature, and the motive for poetry, a motive that Lowell portrays himself as inheriting from these Quakers, from Thoreau, Melville, American Calvinism, Roman Catholicism, the whole national experience. Lowell had recently published in *Partisan Review* a version of "Quaker Graveyard" that Jarrell had much admired, and in the sheaf of poems sent to Texas, Lowell included an offprint of the published poem. But Lowell was by no means done with it, either at that time or a decade after. He also sent along three new sections that expanded the poem considerably, bringing it to a total of eight parts. Twenty-five years later, the revisions were moving in the opposite direction, for in the version published in the *Selected Poems* issued in London in 1974, "Quaker Graveyard" has been trimmed down to only four sections, and the two "Our Lady of Walsingham" stanzas, which served as the central interlude, the eye of the storm in 1945, are set off as a completely separate poem. The point is that "Quaker Graveyard" was a career-long process; what came and went in it reflected Lowell's evolving conception of the range and reach of his own poetry, his shifting idea of how much could be set afloat on the broad, unstable metaphor of the sea, how successfully these stormy waters and his own rhetorical skills could keep a near-miscellany of perceptions and vignettes in some kind of unity. On this poem Jarrell's commentary faced its largest challenge. Having led Lowell in the direction of tautness, focus, precision, Jarrell apparently recognized nonetheless that what was at stake in this longer work was different, that this was one of those rhapsodies in which the poet had to be given his head. Jarrell's own best role now was to keep silent, except about those crises when sheer bulk and heterogeneity moved the poem close to collapse. The commentary in the margins of the *Partisan Review* offprint is chiefly praise, the firm suggestions having to do with minor word-choices and punctuation. It was in the new stanzas, rather, that Jarrell found the poem in trouble. A new section 3 was marred by a flat ending:

> I have heard their cry:
> "If God Himself had not been on our side,
> If God Himself had not been on our side,
> When the Atlantic rose against us, why,
> Then it had swallowed us up quick."
> And then the waters overwhelmed us, slick
> And salt went over our souls,
> The waters of the proud went over our souls.

In the new section 5 Lowell was having serious problems in both language and intractable subject matter. From the extant typescripts:

> When you were children, the northeasters ripped
> The rotten canvas from your model-boats
> And Bremen dinghys in Nantucket. What
> You were was camouflaged in spangled coats,
> But the blank salvos of Versailles had stripped
> You in their bluster and your teeth were cut
> On a barbaric broom-pole's butt,
> Churning into your thin
> Blue-blooded chin;
> There was cold steel behind the horseplay. But
> Even your stolid prescience sensed the time
> Was ripe to take a broom
> And clear this room
> Our vestibule to crime:
>
> Recall the shadows its doll-curtains rained
> On Mary Winslow's breakfast set from blue
> Canton, the breaking of the haggard tide
> On the gigantic print of Waterloo,—
> The blacks and whites obscurely waterstained,
> With a curled scar across the glass. You cried
> To see Napoleon's eagle-standard slide
> From the gloved cuirassier,
> Staff officer

And the new section 7 began:

> And now that the long smother snaps your spine
> Across Poseidon's shins
> To banquet the disgusting gulls and terns
> Of the debauched Atlantic, Sailor, and spins
> Your green-eyed liquefaction to the sterns
> Of the ships of the line
> At drydock; will the sun,
> Descending, harnessed, harassed, huge
> Horse up the ocean, spun,
> In the fiery deluge,
> World-wide?

What is remarkable about Jarrell's response to all this is that he is insistent, yet in a way restrained: while arguing that the poem needed a good cleaning-out, he does not himself stifle "Quaker Graveyard" with too much thematic definition:

> I like all of the new III except the waters of the proud, which doesn't seem effective enough or being *so*: the Quakers weren't notably proud, were they? I think the new Stanza V with Versailles and Napoleon a *great* mistake: it takes you out of the world of the poem, is too didactic ("time was ripe to take a broom and clear this room our vestibule to crime") brings in bric a brac that doesn't fit, and generally weakens and dissipates the effect of the whole poem. I beg you to leave it out. *And* to leave out VII, which seems overwritten, too rhetorical, not really functioning in the poem. "Snaps your spine across Poisedon's *shine*" [*sic*] seems too calculated to shock, along with the *disgusting* gulls and *debauched* Atlantic. Then look at all this extreme rhetoric: green-eyed liquefaction; fiery deluge, corrosive smoulder of its world; the knock and knowledge of the rainbow's fouled/and halcyon summer; loud-mouthed terror howled; time's lubricious feathers. And this seems awfully contrived and rhetorical, a tour de force but awkward too.

Versailles and Napoleon disappeared in due course from "Quaker Graveyard," the overwritten new section 7 likewise never saw print, and the new 3, when it appeared in *Lord Weary's Castle*, was strengthened by the cutting of the two closing lines. The whole poem came through these revisions with one more section than the *Partisan Review* version, but with more intensity: the one new section to pass both Lowell's and Jarrell's scrutiny is in fact the strongest evocation of that graveyard.

"The Quaker Graveyard in Nantucket" may have had a narrow escape; but like the whole of *Lord Weary's Castle* it remains from start to finish the work of one hand, Robert Lowell's. If in a sense Randall Jarrell is constantly present in the book, his presence scrupulously confines itself to the sidelines; what is most notable in this correspondence is the delicacy with which he commented. Lowell's voice had to find its own best pitch and steadiness; it required, and received, only lean, firm guidance away from those sins of excess which Lowell's brand of genius was always heir to. Jarrell's efforts for the book did not of course stop here; he helped Lowell find a publisher for it, reviewed or endorsed it in print several times in the years following its appearance. But nothing Jarrell might have done for Lowell's career detracts from Lowell's achievement in *Lord Weary's Castle*—or from Jarrell's own integrity and clearheadedness, his private achievement as a critic in the highest sense of the word. Having worked behind the scenes with such restraint, and to such good effect, Jarrell had a right to lead national applause for a book that not only his own words, but his own measured silences had helped keep its promise. These letters, these marginal comments, offer a lesson in when to speak and when to keep quiet as a critic, even when working with the closest of friends; and Jarrell's splendid balance of trenchancy and circumspection, a balance that shows itself almost everywhere in his letters about *Lord Weary's Castle*, must figure in our thinking about his overall achievement, our estimation of his range, his powers, and the role he played in bringing about the expression of the postwar mind.

Chronology

1917   Robert Traill Spence Lowell, Jr., is born in Boston on March 1, the only child of Commander R. T. S. Lowell and Charlotte Winslow.

1924–30   Lowell attends Brimmer School in Boston.

1930–35   Lowell attends St. Mark's School in Southborough, Massachusetts. There he acquires his nickname, "Cal" (after Caligula). During his senior year he studies with Richard Eberhart.

1935–37   Lowell studies at Harvard. During the summer he lives with Allen Tate and his wife Caroline Gordon at their home in Clarkesville, Tennessee. Also at the Tates' was Ford Madox Ford.

1937–40   Lowell transfers to Kenyon College in Ohio, where he studies with John Crowe Ransom. His friends there include Randall Jarrell and Peter Taylor. Lowell graduates *summa cum laude* with a classics major. On April 2, 1940, he marries the novelist Jean Stafford.

1940–41   Lowell teaches English at Kenyon and takes graduate courses at Louisiana State University under Cleanth Brooks and Robert Penn Warren.

1941–42   Sheed & Ward, a Roman Catholic publishing house in New York City, employs Lowell as an editorial assistant.

1942–43   Returning to live with the Tates, Lowell writes *Land of Unlikeness*. In 1943 he is convicted for failure to obey the Selective Service Act and serves about half of a one-year-and-one-day sentence in the federal prison in Danbury, Connecticut.

1944   *Land of Unlikeness* is published in July by the Cummington Press. After living briefly in Maine, Lowell moves to New York City.

1946   *Lord Weary's Castle* is published by Harcourt, Brace and wins the Pulitzer Prize.

1947   Lowell is awarded a Guggenheim Fellowship and the American Academy of Arts and Letters Prize. He also serves as Poetry Consultant to the Library of Congress.

1948   In June, Lowell divorces Jean Stafford.

1949   Lowell serves on the prize committee for the first Bollingen Prize, which is awarded to Ezra Pound for the *Pisan Cantos*. In March, the poet is hospitalized for a nervous breakdown; for the rest of his life he suffers from manic-depressive bouts. On July 28, he marries writer Elizabeth Hardwick.

1950   British publisher Faber & Faber brings out *Poems 1938–49*. Lowell teaches at the University of Iowa and at Kenyon. His father dies.

1950–53   The poet lives and travels in Europe.

1951   *The Mills of the Kavanaughs* is published.

1953–54   Lowell teaches at Iowa along with John Berryman, and among his students is W. D. Snodgrass. He also teaches at the University of Indiana and at the University of Cincinnati. During this time he begins a correspondence with poet William Carlos Williams. In February 1954 his mother dies.

1954–60   Lowell moves to Boston, and teaches at Boston University for the last five years of this period. Among his students are Anne Sexton, Sylvia Plath, and George Starbuck.

1957   Lowell's first child, Harriet Winslow, is born in January. From March through April, he undertakes a speaking tour on the West Coast.

1959   *Life Studies* is published and wins the National Book Award. He also shares the Guinness Poetry Award with W. H. Auden and Edith Sitwell.

1960   The Ford Foundation awards Lowell a grant to work as poet-librettist with the Metropolitan Opera and the New York City

Opera. On June 5 he reads "For the Union Dead" aloud on the Boston Common during the Boston Festival of the Arts.

1960–70   The Lowells live in New York City.

1961   *Imitations* is published. Although it receives mixed reviews, it is awarded the Bollingen Translation Prize as well as the Harriet Monroe Memorial Prize. Lowell's version of Racine's *Phaedra* is published.

1963–67   Lowell teaches at Harvard, which gives him a lifelong appointment.

1964   *For the Union Dead* is published. Two of the three plays published as *The Old Glory* are produced at the American Place Theatre in New York City. One of the plays, *Benito Cereno*, wins an Obie for the best off-Broadway play.

1965   In protest against the Vietnam War, Lowell publicly declines an invitation from President Lyndon B. Johnson to attend the White House Festival of the Arts.

1967   *Near the Ocean* is published. Lowell becomes writer-in-residence at the Yale School of Drama, where his *Prometheus Bound* is produced. Also during this year, Lowell participates in the anti-Vietnam War march on the Pentagon.

1968   A revised edition of *The Old Glory* is published. Lowell campaigns for Eugene McCarthy in the Democratic primaries.

1969   *Notebook 1967–68* and *Prometheus Bound* are published.

1970   *Notebook* (revised and expanded) is published. Lowell is named a Visiting Fellow at All Souls College, Oxford.

1970–76   Lowell lives in England; from 1970 to 1972 he teaches at Essex University.

1971   Robert Sheridan is born to Lowell and Caroline Blackwood.

1972   Lowell is divorced from Elizabeth Hardwick and, in October, marries Caroline Blackwood.

1973   *The Dolphin, History*, and *For Lizzie and Harriet* are published. *The Dolphin* wins the Pulitzer Prize.

1974   *Robert Lowell's Poems: A Selection* is published. The poet receives the Copernicus Award for lifetime achievement in poetry.

1976   *Selected Poems* is published.

1977   *Day by Day* is published and is awarded the National Book
        Critics Circle Award. Lowell receives the American Academy
        and Institute of Arts and Letters National Medal for Litera-
        ture. He returns to the U.S. and spends the summer with
        Elizabeth Hardwick. On September 12, Lowell dies at the age
        of sixty in New York City.

1978   Lowell's translation of the *Oresteia of Aeschylus* is published
        posthumously.

Contributors

HAROLD BLOOM, Sterling Professor of the Humanities at Yale University, is the author of *The Anxiety of Influence, Poetry and Repression*, and many other volumes of literary criticism. His forthcoming study, *Freud: Transference and Authority*, attempts a full-scale reading of all of Freud's major writings. A MacArthur Prize Fellow, he is general editor of five series of literary criticism published by Chelsea House.

HUGH B. STAPLES teaches comparative literature at the University of Cincinnati.

JOHN SIMON, the noted film and drama critic, has written many articles and numerous books on both American and foreign productions.

GABRIEL PEARSON is a British critic whose publications include *Dickens and the Twentieth Century*, which he edited with John J. Gross.

DAVID BROMWICH, Professor of English at Princeton University, is author of *Hazlitt: The Mind of a Critic*. He has forthcoming a book on modern American poetry.

DWIGHT EDDINS, Professor of English at the University of Alabama, is author of *Yeats: The Nineteenth Century Matrix*.

FRANCES FERGUSON teaches at the University of California, Berkeley. She is author of *Wordsworth: Language as Counter-Spirit*.

STEPHEN YENSER is Professor of English at the University of California, Los Angeles.

DAVID KALSTONE teaches at Rutgers. His books include *Five Temperaments: Elizabeth Bishop, Robert Lowell, James Merrill, Adrienne Rich, John Ashbery* and *Sidney's Poetry*.

HELEN VENDLER is Professor of English at Boston University and Harvard University. She is author of several books; the most recent is *The Odes of John Keats*. She has also written on Wallace Stevens, Yeats, and Herbert.

STEVEN GOULD AXELROD is Associate Professor of English at the University of California, Riverside. He has published two books on Lowell, one in collaboration with Helen Deese: *Robert Lowell: A Reference Guide*.

NEIL CORCORAN is the author of *The Song of Deeds: A Study of the Anathemata of David Jones*.

BRUCE MICHELSON, Associate Professor of English at the University of Illinois, has published criticism on Hawthorne, Edith Wharton, Robert Lowell, and Richard Wilbur.

Bibliography

Agenda 18, no. 3 (Autumn 1980). Special Robert Lowell issue.

Alvarez, A. "Robert Lowell in Conversation." *Review* 8 (August 1963): 36–40.

———. "Talk with Robert Lowell." *Encounter* 24 (February 1965): 39–43. Reprinted in *Under Pressure*. New York: Penguin, 1966.

Anzilotti, Rolando. *Robert Lowell: A Tribute*. Pisa: Nistri-Lischi Editori, 1979.

Axelrod, Steven G. "Robert Lowell and the New York Intellectuals." *English Language Notes* 11, no. 3 (March 1974): 206–9.

———. "Lowell's *The Dolphin* as a 'Book of Life.' " *Contemporary Literature* 18, no. 4 (Autumn 1977): 458–74.

Barry, Jackson G. "Robert Lowell's 'Confessional' Image of an Age: Theme and Language in Poetic Form." *Ariel* 12, no. 1 (January 1981): 51–57.

Bayley, John. "Robert Lowell: The Poetry of Cancellation." *London Magazine* 6 (June 1966): 76–85.

———. "The Morality of Form in the Poetry of Robert Lowell." *Ariel* 9, no. 1 (January 1978): 3–17.

———. "Moment after Moment: *Day by Day* by Robert Lowell." In *Selected Essays*, 45–50. Cambridge: Cambridge University Press, 1984.

Bell, Vereen M. *Robert Lowell: Nihilist as Hero*. Cambridge: Harvard University Press, 1983.

Berryman, John. "Robert Lowell and Others." In *The Freedom of the Poet*, 286–96. New York: Farrar, Straus & Giroux, 1976.

Bewley, Marius. "Some Aspects of American Poetry." In *The Complex Fate*. London: Chatto & Windus, 1952.

Blackmur, R. P. *Form & Value in Modern Poetry*. New York: Doubleday Anchor, 1957.

Brustein, Robert. "Introduction (1965)." In *The Old Glory* by Robert Lowell, 215–18. New York: Farrar, Straus & Giroux, 1968.

Carruth, Hayden. "A Meaning of Robert Lowell." *Hudson Review* 20 (Autumn 1967): 429–47.

Cohen, B. Bernard. "Tragic Vision in the Sixties." *Genre* 3, no. 3 (September 1970): 254–71.

Cooper, Philip. *The Autobiographical Myth of Robert Lowell*. Chapel Hill: University of North Carolina Press, 1970.

Cosgrave, Patrick. *The Public Poetry of Robert Lowell*. New York: Taplinger Publications, 1972.

Donoghue, Denis. *Connoisseurs of Chaos: Ideas of Order in Modern American Poetry*. New York: Columbia University Press, 1984.

Dubrow, Heather. "The Marine in the Garden: Pastoral Elements in Lowell's 'Quaker Graveyard.' " *Philological Quarterly* 62, no. 2 (Spring 1983): 127–45.

Dunn, Douglas. "The Big Race: Lowell's Visions and Revisions." *Encounter* 41, no. 4 (October 1973): 107–13.

Ehrenpreis, Irvin. "The Age of Lowell." In *American Poetry*. London: Edward Arnold, 1965.

Fein, Richard J. *Robert Lowell*. New York: Twayne, 1970.

———. *"Lord Weary's Castle* Revisited." *PMLA* 89, no. 1 (January 1974): 34–41.

———. "Looking for Robert Lowell in Boston." *The Literary Review* 21, no. 3 (Spring 1978): 285–303.

Fraser, G. S. "Near the Ocean." *Salmagundi* 37 (Spring 1977): 73–87.

Fried, Michael. "The Achievement of Robert Lowell." *London Magazine* 2 (October 1967): 54–64.

Furia, Philip. " 'IS, the whited monster': Lowell's Quaker Graveyard Revisited." *Texas Studies in Literature and Language* 17, no. 4 (Winter 1976): 837–54.

Haffenden, John. "The Last Parnassian: Robert Lowell." *Agenda* 16, no. 2 (Summer 1978): 40–46.

Hamilton, Ian. *Robert Lowell: A Biography*. New York: Random House, 1982.

———. "Robert Lowell." In *The Modern Poet*, edited by Ian Hamilton, 32–41. New York: Horizon Press, 1968.

Hardison, O. B. "Robert Lowell: The Poet and the World's Body." *Shenandoah* 14 (Winter 1963): 24–32.

Hass, Robert. "Lowell's Graveyard." *Salmagundi* 37 (Spring 1977): 56–72.

Hollander, John. "Robert Lowell's New Book." *Poetry* 95, no. 1 (October 1959): 41–46.

Holloway, John. "Robert Lowell and the Public Dimension." *Encounter* 30 (April 1968): 73–79.

Jarrell, Randall. *Poetry and the Age*. New York: Vintage, 1959.

Kazin, Alfred. "Robert Lowell and John Ashbery: The Difference between Poets." *Esquire* (January 1978): 20–22.

Kunitz, Stanley. "Talk with Robert Lowell." *New York Times Book Review* (October 4, 1964): 34.

Lane, Lauriate, Jr. "Robert Lowell: The Problems and Power of Allusion." *Dalhousie Review* 60, no. 4 (Winter 1980–81): 697–702.

London, Michael, and Robert Boyers, eds. *Robert Lowell: A Portrait of the Artist in His Time*. New York: David Lewis Publishers, 1970.

Mailer, Norman. "The Liberal Party." In *Armies of the Night*, 13–29. New York: New American Library, 1968.

Martin, Jay. *Robert Lowell*. Minneapolis: University of Minnesota Press, 1970.

———. "Robert Lowell." In *Seven American Poets from MacLeish to Nemerov*, edited by Denis Donoghue, 209–49. Minneapolis: University of Minnesota Press, 1975.

Mazzaro, Jerome. *The Poetic Themes of Robert Lowell*. Ann Arbor: University of Michigan Press, 1965.

———. "Robert Lowell's Early Politics of Apocalypse." In *Modern American Poetry:*

Essays in Criticism, edited by Jerome Mazzaro, 321–50. New York: David McKay, 1970.

———. *"Prometheus Bound:* Robert Lowell and Aeschylus." *Comparative Drama* 7, no. 4 (Winter 1973–74): 278–90.

McFadden, George. *"Life Studies*—Robert Lowell's Comic Breakthrough." *PMLA* 90, no. 1 (January 1975): 96–106.

Meiners, R. K. *Everything to Be Endured: An Essay on Robert Lowell and Modern Poetry.* Columbia: University of Missouri Press, 1970.

Ong, Walter J. *In the Human Grain.* New York: Macmillan, 1967.

Parkinson, Thomas. *Robert Lowell: A Collection of Critical Essays.* Englewood Cliffs, N.J.: Prentice-Hall, Inc., 1968.

Peck, John. "Reflections of Lowell's 'Domesday Book.' " *Salmagundi* 37 (Spring 1977): 32–36.

Perloff, Marjorie. "Death by Water: The Winslow Elegies of Robert Lowell." *Journal of English Literary History* 34 (March 1967): 116–40.

———. "Realism and the Confessional Mode of Robert Lowell." *Contemporary Literature* 11, no. 4 (Autumn 1970): 470–87.

———. *The Poetic Art of Robert Lowell.* Ithaca, N.Y.: Cornell University Press, 1973.

Pinsker, Sanford. "John Berryman and Robert Lowell: The Middle Generation, Reconsidered." *The Literary Review* 27, no. 2 (Winter 1984): 252–61.

Pinsky, Robert. "The Conquered Kings of Robert Lowell." *Salmagundi* 37 (Spring 1977): 102–5.

———. *The Situation of Poetry: Contemporary Poetry and Its Traditions.* Princeton, N.J.: Princeton University Press, 1976.

Price, Jonathan, ed. *Critics on Robert Lowell.* Coral Gables, Fla.: University of Miami Press, 1972.

———. "The Making of *Prometheus Bound.*" *Yale Alumni Magazine* (June 1967): 30–37.

Procopiow, Norma. *"Day by Day:* Lowell's Poetic of Imitation." *Ariel* 14, no. 1 (January 1983): 5–14.

Rosenthal, M. L. *The New Poets.* New York: Oxford University Press, 1967.

———. *The Modern Poets: A Critical Introduction.* New York: Oxford University Press, 1960.

Rosenthal, M. L., and Sally M. Gall. *The Modern Poetic Sequence: The Genius of Modern Poetry.* New York: Oxford University Press, 1983.

Rudman, Mark. *Robert Lowell: An Introduction to the Poetry.* New York: Columbia University Press, 1983.

Salmagundi 37 (Spring 1977). Special Robert Lowell issue.

Schechter, Joel. "Lowell Offstage." Review of *The Oresteia. The Nation* (May 19, 1979): 576–78.

Segal, Erich. "The Oresteia of Aeschylus by Robert Lowell." *The New Republic* (June 30, 1979): 32–35.

Seidel, Frederick. "Interview with Robert Lowell." *Paris Review* 25 (Winter–Spring 1961): 56–95.

Shaw, Robert B. "Lowell in the Seventies." *Contemporary Literature* 23, no. 4 (Fall 1982): 515–27.

Simon, John. "Abuse of Privilege: Lowell as Translator." *Hudson Review* 20 (Winter 1967–68): 543–62.

Smith, Vivian. *The Poetry of Robert Lowell.* Sydney: Sydney University Press, 1974.

Snodgrass, W. D. "In Praise of Robert Lowell." Review of *The Old Glory*. *The New York Review of Books* (December 3, 1964): 8–10.

Staples, Hugh B. *Robert Lowell: The First Twenty Years*. New York: Farrar, Straus & Cudahy, 1962.

Stepanchev, Stephen. "Robert Lowell." In *American Poetry since 1945*. New York: Harper & Row, 1965.

Tate, Allen. "Robert Lowell." *Harvard Advocate* 145 (November 1961): 5.

Tulip, James. "The Poetic Voices of Robert Lowell." *Poetry Australia* 39 (April 1971): 49–57.

Williams, William Carlos. *Selected Essays*. New York: New Directions, 1969.

Williamson, Alan. *Pity the Monsters: The Political Vision of Robert Lowell*. New Haven: Yale University Press, 1974.

————. "The Reshaping of 'Waking Early Sunday Morning.' " *Agenda* 18, no. 3 (Autumn 1980): 47–62.

Acknowledgments

"*Land of Unlikeness*" by Hugh B. Staples from *Robert Lowell: The First Twenty Years* by Hugh B. Staples, © 1962 by Hugh B. Staples. Reprinted by permission of the author and Farrar, Straus & Giroux, Inc.

"Strange Devices on the Banner" by John Simon from *Robert Lowell: A Portrait of the Artist in His Time*, edited by Michael London and Robert Boyers, © 1970 by David Lewis Publisher, Inc. Reprinted by permission.

"The Middle Years" (originally entitled "Robert Lowell: The Middle Years") by Gabriel Pearson from *Contemporary Poetry in America: Essays and Interviews*, edited by Robert Boyers, © 1974 by Robert Boyers. Reprinted by permission of the editor and Schocken Books, Inc.

"*Notebook*" (originally entitled "Reading Robert Lowell") by David Bromwich from *Commentary* 52, no. 2 (August 1971), © 1971 by the American Jewish Committee. Reprinted by permission.

"Poet and State in the Verse of Robert Lowell" by Dwight Eddins from *Texas Studies in Literature and Language* 15, no. 2 (Summer 1973), © 1973 by the University of Texas Press. Reprinted by permission of the author and the publisher.

"Appointments with Time: Robert Lowell's Poetry through the *Notebooks*" by Frances Ferguson from *American Poetry since 1960: Some Critical Perspectives*, edited by Robert B. Shaw, © 1973 by Frances Ferguson. Reprinted by permission of the author and Carcanet Press Ltd.

"*Imitations*" (originally entitled "Many Personalities, One Voice: *Imitations* (1961)") by Stephen Yenser from *Circle to Circle: The Poetry of Robert Lowell* by Stephen Yenser © 1975 by the Regents of the University of California. Reprinted by permission of the University of California Press.

"The Uses of History" (originally entitled "Robert Lowell: The Uses of History") by David Kalstone from *Five Temperaments* by David Kalstone, © 1977 by David Kalstone. Reprinted by permission of the author and Oxford University Press.

"Last Days and Last Poems" (originally entitled "Robert Lowell") by Helen Vendler from *Part of Nature, Part of Us: Modern American Poetry* by Helen Vendler, © 1980 by the President and Fellows of Harvard College. Reprinted by permission of Harvard University Press.

"Starting Over: Learning from Williams" (originally entitled "Photographs of Experience") by Steven Gould Axelrod from *Robert Lowell: Life and Art* by Steven Gould Axelrod, © 1978 by Princeton University Press. Reprinted by permission of Princeton University Press.

"Lowell *Retiarius:* Towards *The Dolphin*" by Neil Corcoran from *Agenda* 18, no. 3 (Autumn 1980), © 1980 by Neil Corcoran. Reprinted by permission.

"Randall Jarrell and Robert Lowell: The Making of *Lord Weary's Castle*" by Bruce Michelson from *Contemporary Literature* 26, no. 4 (Winter 1985), © 1985 by the Board of Regents of the University of Wisconsin System. Reprinted by permission of the University of Wisconsin Press.

Index

175